Kingdom BUILDER'S MINDSET

Renewing Minds to Live Transformed and Victorious Lives – A 40-Day Guide

DANIELA BLAKE

COPYRIGHT & CREDITS

ISBN 978-976-96737-0-0 (pb) 978-976-96737-1-7 (eb)

ISSN: 0799-6659

Cover design: Geek Resource Centre

Published by: THE PUBLISHER'S NOTEBOOK LIMITED

Email: thepublishersnotebook@gmail.com

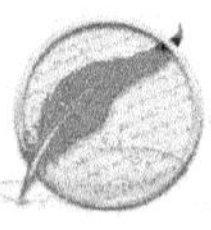

2021

DEDICATION

This book is dedicated to broken people.

Like myself, who has lived a life faced with many rigorous challenges, I write to all those people (both young and old) going through or have gone through life's difficulties. Those who are afraid to speak up about the things you struggle or have struggled with, I share some of my experiences through this guide that you will know you are not alone.

TABLE OF CONTENTS

PREFACE

When I was a teenager, I kept diaries hidden all over my home in secret places. My diaries were a place to confess my secrets, struggles, and fears without judgment or punishment. It felt good to get all of those thoughts and feelings out of my head and down on paper. For me, the world seemed clearer. I never dreamt of becoming a writer. For all I know, I never thought that I had it in me. Growing up, I have always been fascinated by books, and from a tender age, I developed a love for reading. As the years grew by, I found myself jotting down thoughts that crept their way into my mind. What started as jotting became full-on journaling. You may ask yourself, what exactly is journaling? It is simply writing down your thoughts and feelings to understand them more clearly. Growing up, I never had an open relationship with my siblings or my parents. The only persons I would talk to about the things I was going through were my friends, and I still did not tell them everything.

Now and then, I would write how I feel. There were no fancy words or careful diligence to formulate metaphorical sentences, just the raw, undiluted expressions of my feelings. Journaling was my savior, and my pen and notebook were my tools of escape from the complexities of reality. In high school, I remember my English teacher telling me that I have a gift for writing. Of course, I did not take her seriously because I did not believe in myself enough to accept what she saw in me. In my lifetime, I have faced innumerable challenges. I have experienced and have been exposed to quite a lot from an early age. I could not tell anyone most of the things I went through at that time, so I decided to write a poetry book to express myself. I did this before I accepted the Lord Jesus Christ as my savior. When I was not yet saved, I was living a life of stress. I was overwhelmed by depression, often with continuous thoughts of suicide. I did not trust anybody, so I kept this all to myself, wearing my best smiles every day to conceal my brokenness. Hey! Know this; I could not hide how I felt some of the times, and my expression would manifest from a deep-seated anger.

After my encounter with the Lord that led to the saving of my soul, I sat at the dining table where I always write. There, I prayed a prayer to God, committing my writing to Him and asking Him to bless all that I write and will write for His glory, and that I may do so under the unction of the anointing. To this date, He has been faithful to answer my prayer. I came to a better understanding of the concept of journaling since I got saved. Spending time in prayer and fasting opened a dam in me flooding with spiritual revelations fresh from heaven. God would put things into my spirit, and I would have to stop what I am doing to write it down. It still happens, and I have realized that this is how the Lord speaks to me. Everything that I faced, whatever I feel, is written in a book. If you search through my room and my books, there is a jotting somewhere. Prayers, poems, speeches, sermons, revelations, you name it.

I found my comfort in writing, and it drove me to this phase in my life where the Lord led me to go a little further by writing this book. It was last year, mid-summer 2020, while I was in one of the darkest seasons in my life, dealing with different issues one after the other, that I started journaling. What made this different was that each time something happened to me, I received a word from it, and scriptures started pouring in like rain to seal the word I received. Each time this happened, I wrote it down until I ended up with over 30 entries. One evening, the Lord impressed upon me to write a book. The fact that the Lord wanted me to do this was very hard for me because I did not think I had it in me to make such a bold step. Nevertheless, I decided to obey. I prayed about this step that God wanted me to take, I also spoke to two of my good friends, and of course, as expected they believed in me and encouraged me to follow God's leading to turn my journal notes into a book.

The writing process for this book was very intense. It involved a lot of prayer and pleading to God as well as a lot of research. Because like Gideon I really wanted to make sure that God wanted me to do this. By the way, I did not fleece God, but I followed the promptings of my heart. God provided me with the wisdom and inspiration to write all that you will read. I marvel each time I take up my manuscript and read the contents within. I am taken aback by the sheer awesomeness of God to have downloaded all this revelation in me. Despite the many times I was faced with the condemning thoughts of whether my book would be good enough or if it will ever be a blessing to someone, I decide that the only way I will know is to face my fears head on by putting this book out there. I can truly say that this has been one of the best writing experiences in my lifetime. As an upcoming Christian author, to be exposed to the nakedness of the writing process has caused me to grow in many ways.

Throughout the process, I have had to deal with both the positive and negative thoughts that plagued me about my writing. I faced days when I had a writer's block and personal concerns when I had my work critiqued by others. I did hours of research, I compared my work to others, I felt inadequate, there were days when I lost inspiration, I fought the urge to give up, and thought I was not qualified to write among other things. Nonetheless I still believe that the process will yield its blessings in due time. As a young Christian, time would not permit me to speak of the things I have gone through in my life, many of which were strategically designed to kill me. Sexual abuse, abandonment, depression, sexual promiscuity, low self-esteem, heartbreak, to name a few. Through it all, I have been victorious. I dare not take any credit for the battles I have won but to give God all the praise, glory, and honor.

He is the sole reason I am alive today with the confidence, boldness, and faith to write about my experiences and share them with the world. ***Kingdom Builder's Mindset** is a 40-day guide to help reshape how we view and deal with the negative circumstances of life using the Word of God.* It is my personal belief that we fail our tests and lose our battles because we are clothed with all our armor except the most important one – the sword of the spirit, which is the Word of God. After many losses, embarrassments, defeats, failed tests, and succumbing to temptations, I realized that I was fighting a war without the appropriate battle gears. As such, I was eventually losing each time I went up against the enemy of my soul.

After withdrawing myself to do some self-introspection, I realized how much I lacked God's Word. I fell short. I lost my battles because I did not know the word to speak in my seasons of tests and trials. Jesus fasted 40 days and night. After which, He was in a terrible condition physically. The devil tempted Him, but He overcame because He knew the right words to speak that would drive the devil away during that time in His life. He rightly said,

> *"It is written, Man shall not live by bread alone, but by every word that proceedeth out of the mouth of God (**Matthew 4:4 KJV**).*

If you desire to live a victorious life, you can certainly achieve it..

> *How can a young man stay pure? Only by living in the word of God and walking in its truth (**Psalms 119:9 TPT**).*

> *And they overcame him by the blood of the Lamb, and by the word of their testimony; and they loved not their lives unto the death (**Revelation 12:11 KJV**).*

You do not have to live in fear. Let me help you find your voice through this book to take a stand to be victorious. As I share some of my experiences and words of encouragement, my sincere prayer is that whoever reads this book will never be the same. Too many people regardless of age, die slowly and silently because of their struggles. Many are hurt, broken, lost, and afraid. They are afraid to talk about what is affecting them or share their experiences to help others because of fear of criticism. Too many of our young people have left the church because we did not take the time to suffer-long or bear with them through their many difficulties and mistakes made. Instead, we extended the cold hand of judgment and resentment, not remembering where we are coming from. Our actions cause them to lose faith in the church, be angry with God and leave His presence only to plunge themselves into further sin.

It pains my heart to see my fellow brothers and sisters in Christ - especially young people - living in sin. My heart goes out to you. I know the pressure. I empathize with your pain, I understand the needs, desires, and longings, but we cannot let our guards down. No, we must not give up on God. He will not give up on you. He is well able to see us through.

ACKNOWLEDGEMENTS

My precious kingdom family, what an exhilarating journey it has been. One, which I believe, was fitting for such a time as this. First, I would like to thank God. I never knew I had it in me to go the length of writing a book. Somebody say, *"but God."* But God knows my heart and is greater than all things. He understood who I am. He saw within me what I never could be able to see in myself and pushed me into what I believe to be my purpose. In the process of putting this book together, I realized how true this gift of writing is for me. God has given me the power to believe in my passion and pursue my dreams. I could never have done this without the faith I have in the Almighty Mighty God.

To my mentor, spiritual father, and friend Gerald Stewart: you were the first person to read and critique my manuscript. Your feedback and suggestions were very much received and incorporated into this masterpiece. I want to say thank you for believing in me, encouraging and being a part of this journey from the start to the finish.

There's a friend that sticks closer than a brother, and I am very humbled to have Shane Harrison as that friend. Throughout the most difficult period in my life and dealing with the loss of my sister, I still had to be working on my book's compilation by doing corrections and rewriting. I was really feeling stressed during that time but Shane you have stood by me in prayer, and you continually encouraged me to push on through that difficult season. Thank you.

To all those who shared their words of encouragements, prayers, gave their financial support and love, thank you.

I would like to extend thanks to Andrew Barton, Kenrick Ash, Kenton Phillips, and Michelle Joseph for your invaluable contribution, encouragements and advice that you have given to me throughout the whole process of putting together this book.

To my entire church family, a big thanks for your encouragement, support, prayers, and belief in me.

Thanks to everyone on the team of The Publisher's Notebook Limited who helped me so much. Special thanks to Sylvia, the patient CEO, and to those who made this book a reality. I recommend The Publisher's Notebook Limited to anyone who is interested in writing and publishing their book. They are so much more than a publishing empire. They are a family.

Special thanks to my brother who I prefer to remain nameless. You motivate and inspire me every day. For your contribution and support to the success of this book I thank you.

LASTLY, TO MY MOM WHOM I LOVE SO DEARLY AND THE REST OF MY FAMILY THANK YOU.

INTRODUCTION

*Do not be conformed to this world, but be transformed by the renewing of your mind, that you may prove what is the good and acceptable and perfect will of God. (**Romans 12:2 KJV**)*

To be an effective Kingdom Ambassador, it is important for you to have a Kingdom Mindset. Having a kingdom mentality propels you to live, act, and lead an effective life here on this earth.

You may ask, what is a Kingdom Mindset? Let us break it down for us to further understand.

Kingdom: - The spiritual realm over which God reigns as king, or the fulfillment on earth of God's will. Kingdom speaks to the rule of God, the territory governed by God, the realm in which God's will, purposes, plans, and desires are fulfilled.

Mindset: - A mindset is your collection of thoughts and beliefs that shape your thought habits. And your thought habits affect how you think, what you feel, and what you do. Your mindset impacts how you make sense of the world, and how you make sense of you. (Source: https://sourcesofinsight.com/what-is-mindset.)

To give a more generalized definition to Kingdom Mindset we can therefore say that *it is a mindset that is focused on Christ more than anything or anyone else. Every thought is shaped with His presence in mind. Getting even more practical, it means considering what Jesus thinks about things more than how we think.*

Colossians 3:2 tells us that we should set our minds on things above, not on earthly things. It is against this backdrop as children of God that we should understand that being born-again means adapting a new way and approach to how we think and do things.

Ephesians 4:21-23 tells us that:

> [21] *Since you have heard about Jesus and have learned the truth that comes from him, [22] throw off your old sinful nature and your former way of life, which is corrupted by lust and deception. [23] Instead, let the Spirit renew your thoughts and attitudes. (NLT)*

Life will deal us a variety of cards that will reflect different types of struggles, tests, trials, and circumstances that are sometimes beyond our control. It does become overwhelming and hard at times to the extent that we would want to give up. Some of us have given up. Over the years, we see where persons have resorted to suicide, drugs, murder, alcoholism, and many other things as a means to an end to relieve them of the situations they face. In moments of adversity, it is easy to adopt a negative mindset and to always think that life is against us. This is not the case for just one set of people, but for every person in existence.

It is important to know that the things of this world are only temporal as are our tests and trials. However, while we are still on this earth, we do not have to succumb to the pressure of the circumstances that we face; neither do we have to think negatively about our situations. Yes! Now it may seem cruel and unfair especially if you are trying your best to live a life that is pleasing to God, but might I remind you that

> *No discipline seems pleasant at the time, but painful. Later on, however, it produces a harvest of righteousness and peace for those who have been trained by it. (Hebrews 12:11 NIV)*

> *Beloved friends, if life gets extremely difficult, with many tests, don't be bewildered as though something strange were overwhelming you. Instead, continue to rejoice, for you, in a measure, have shared in the sufferings of the Anointed One so that you can share in the revelation of his glory*

With that view in mind, it is with great joy and empathy that I share with you what the Lord has done for me and laid on my heart over the years after I was living a life of utter emptiness and darkness. **Kingdom Builder's Mindset** *is a 40-day guide to help reshape how we view and deal with the negative circumstances of life using the Word of God.* The only way I was able to overcome the many dark, lonely, depressing, guilt-ridden, suicidal, and heartbroken seasons in my life was through the transformational power that is found in the Word of God. God brought me to and through a season of darkness, tests, and trials to fully break me to the point where He could use His words to make me over again. I am in a much better place today than I was 5 years ago. It is still an uphill task but with the help of God's Word, which has become a lamp unto my feet and a light unto my path. I can properly see my way through the rough terrains of life by walking by faith and not by sight.

The purpose of this book is to share some of my experiences and to provide a well of encouragement that you can daily drink from to give you added strength and hope to not only survive, but to live through your most difficult days by spending time in the Word of God. Setting yourself to understand His mind, will, purpose and heart towards you and the situations you may face. It is my hope that after you go on this 40 days' journey your minds will be renewed and transformed. I pray that for those who have allowed their situation to steal their voice to speak positive things into being, I pray that through this guide you will find your voice through God's Word to speak those things that are not as though they are in the atmosphere. I pray for a revolution to begin in the spirit of your minds today as we go on this journey to wholeness, purpose, fulfillment, and self-discovery in Jesus Name.

In understanding The Kingdom, here are a few scriptures that tell us how to enter the Kingdom of God, what the Kingdom of God is, what it is NOT and where it can be found.

Entry into the Kingdom of God

- *Jesus answered and said unto him, Verily, verily, I say unto thee, Except a man be born again, he cannot see the kingdom of God. **(John 3:3 KJV)***

- *Jesus answered, Verily, verily, I say unto thee, Except a man be born of water and of the Spirit, he cannot enter into the kingdom of God. **(John 3:5 KJV)***

What is the kingdom of God NOT! and where is the kingdom of God found?

What the Kingdom of God is NOT:

- *For the kingdom of God is not meat and drink; but righteousness, and peace, and joy in the Holy Ghost. **(Romans 14:17 KJV)***

- *For the kingdom of God is not in word, but in power. (1 Corinthians 4:20 KJV)*

Where is the Kingdom of God found?

- *Jesus answered, My kingdom is not of this world: if my kingdom were of this world, then would my servants fight, that I should not be delivered to the Jews: but now is my kingdom not from hence. (John 18:36 KJV)*

- *And when he was demanded of the Pharisees, when the kingdom of God should come, he answered them and said, The kingdom of God cometh not with observation: Neither shall they say, Lo here! or, lo there! for, behold, the kingdom of God is within you. (Luke 17:20-21 KJV)*

Kingdom Builder's Mindset

DAY 1 – AM I NOT ENOUGH?

> **Exodus 4:10 KJV**
>
> And Moses said unto the LORD, O my LORD, I am not eloquent, neither heretofore, nor since thou hast spoken unto thy servant: but I am slow of speech, and of a slow tongue.
>
> And the LORD said unto him, Who hath made man's mouth? or who maketh the dumb, or deaf, or the seeing, or the blind? have not I the LORD?

There are days when we get the feeling of not being enough. Sometimes this happens when we are faced with different tasks or found in situations, highlighting how we come up short or lack the necessary elements, skills, and abilities needed to effectively carry out that task or deal with the problem at hand. Sometimes we feel inadequate when there is a promotion opening at work. Academically, you are not qualified, yet you feel confident that you can excel tremendously in that area if given the opportunity. You could be at school, and you desire to become the head girl or head boy. Still, when you think about your personality as shy and your inability to be outspoken coupled with other underlying weaknesses, you rule yourself out as not being fit for the position.

On the other hand, God could call you to a particular ministry in the church, but when you look at yourself and the state of your life, you somehow believe that you would fail at such a task even if God Himself were the one who bids you to it. There are so many other examples we could explore, but I want you to know that you are not alone, and you are not the only one who has experienced the feeling of inadequacy. God called Moses to deliver the children of Israel out of bondage in Egypt.

Now therefore, behold, the cry of the children of
Israel is come unto me: and I have also seen the

oppression wherewith the Egyptians oppress them. Come now therefore, and I will send thee unto Pharaoh, that thou mayest bring forth my people the children of Israel out of Egypt. And Moses said unto God, Who am I, that I should go unto Pharaoh, and that I should bring forth the children of Israel out of Egypt? **(Exodus 3:9-11 KJV)**

And Moses said unto the Lord, O my Lord, I am not eloquent, neither heretofore, nor since thou hast spoken unto thy servant: but I am slow of speech, and of a slow tongue. And the Lord said unto him, Who hath made man's mouth? or who maketh the dumb, or deaf, or the seeing, or the blind? have not I the Lord? Now therefore go, and I will be with thy mouth, and teach thee what thou shalt say. And he said, O my Lord, send, I pray thee, by the hand of him whom thou wilt send. And the anger of the Lord was kindled against Moses, and he said, Is not Aaron the Levite thy brother? I know that he can speak well. And also, behold, he cometh forth to meet thee: and when he seeth thee, he will be glad in his heart. And thou shalt speak unto him, and put words in his mouth: and I will be with thy mouth, and with his mouth, and will teach you what ye shall do. (Exodus 4:10-15 KJV)

Does this sound like us at any time when faced with similar situations? Yes, I do believe so. Moses was so focused on his inabilities that he allowed it to overshadow the fact that he was conversing with God Himself. He forgot the fantastic sight of the Lord appearing in the likeness of a burning bush and the experience of standing in the presence of great holiness.

"When the Lord saw that he had gone over to look, God called to him from within the bush, "Moses! Moses!" And Moses said, "Here I am." "Do not come any closer," God said. "Take off your sandals, for the place where you are standing is holy ground." Then he said, "I am the God of your father, the God of Abraham, the God of Isaac and the God of Jacob." At this, Moses hid his face, because he was afraid to look at God (Exodus 3:4-5 BSB).

Moses' encounter with the Lord shows how crippling and deadly it can be to focus on our insufficiency and not on God. When I was faced with always feeling like I was never enough, my life was so miserable and unhappy. Every day I would look at the good in other people's lives and find more faults with mine. However, one of the fascinating assurances that give me sweet peace and consolation is the fact that I belong to a God who loves me and accepts me the way I am, even if I view myself as insufficient.

He has borne all my sins and took upon Himself everything I would have and will ever face, including the feeling of not being enough. Did I say that you are not alone? Of a truth, the Bible is our guide, and it tells us all we need to know to live a victorious life through faith in Christ alone. All our worth, value and meaning comes from God and His Word spoken concerning us. Paul says,

> *"Not that we are sufficient in ourselves to claim anything as coming from us, but our sufficiency is from God"* **(2 Corinthians 3:5 ESV).**

There are other truths we can rely on when we feel like we are not enough, such as:

> *"And I am sure of this, that he who began a good work in you will bring it to completion at the day of Jesus Christ* **(Philippians 1:6** *ESV).*

> *But his answer was: "My grace is all you need, for my power is greatest when you are weak." I am most happy, then, to be proud of my weaknesses, to feel the protection of Christ's power over me I am content with weaknesses, insults, hardships, persecutions, and difficulties for Christ's sake. For*

Call to Action

Whenever you get the chance, take some time to listen to this song by the **Brooklyn Tabernacle Choir – More Than Enough.** It puts into perspective that no matter how much you feel like you are not enough, you can rest assured that He (God) is more than enough for you.

DAY 2 - DAYS OF COMPLAINTS

Philippians 2:14-14 KJV

Do all things without murmurings and disputings:

That ye may be blameless and harmless, the sons of God, without rebuke, in the midst of a crooked and perverse nation, among whom ye shine as lights in the world;

Have you ever considered the negative implications of our selfish actions, how badly they can affect others? You would be amazed how far a little kindness and selflessness can go. Life is not all about us, and it is certainly not centered on us or the challenges that we face in life. Living our life is all about how we overcome our many trials through Christ and share our testimonies of the goodness of God to help others who may be facing similar situations. So I think it is high time we wake up and smell the roses. We complain about our lives, what we have and do not have, yet fail to give God thanks. We also fail to recognize that others are in far more desperate positions than we are.

I used to consider myself the number one complainer in the world, extreme! I know. But I would get so upset when I asked for things and did not receive them, or when I prayed to God about something I was confident in myself was in His will for me, whereas I ended up feeling like I was talking to the air because I did not receive from God. I cursed God because other individuals would get the same thing I prayed for, and well, I was jealous even when things didn't go my way or if I thought I was giving too much and never received. All this led me to complain, and I became selfish. All of which is unacceptable to God.

Paul said:

"I know what it is to be in need, and I know what it is to have plenty. I have learned the secret of being content in any and every situation, whether well fed or hungry, whether living in plenty or in want **(Philippians 4:12** *NIV).***

If Paul was able to learn such a valuable lesson, then we too could learn to live as instructed in the following scripture:

"In everything give thanks: for this is the will of God in Christ Jesus concerning us **(1 Thessalonians 5:18 KJV).**

Paul went on to say

"...that we should do all things without murmurings and disputings: That ye may be blameless and harmless, the sons of God, without rebuke, in the midst of a crooked and perverse nation, among whom ye shine as lights in the world; **(Philippians 2:14-15 KJV).**

Jesus came not for the benefit of Himself, neither lived He on account of gaining anything for Himself. He came and lived His life for us so that we could have an example to follow.

We should seek to help others just as Christ did. We should be grateful for what we have and thank God in advance by faith for what He will do. Reach out to someone in need today and stop complaining and living your life selfishly and not to others' benefit. The reason we were made light when we were born-again was not necessarily for us. When our light shines, it lights the path for those walking in darkness to see clearer and find a better way. When we fail to shine our light that the world may see and sit comfortably in our state of ineffectiveness, we act selfishly. We have a purpose to fulfill, and some persons may never read the bible or walk into a church until they see our light through our actions shining, which will help them see clearer and find a better way.

Call to Action

Whenever you are tempted to complain, think about those who are in a far more impoverished position and

And consider the example that Jesus, the Anointed One, has set before us. Let his mindset become your motivation **(Philippians 2:4-5 TPT).**

DAY 3 - DEMANDING PRESSURES OF LIFE

Luke 10: 40 KJV

But Martha was distracted by all the preparations that had to be made. She came to him and asked, "Lord, don't you care that my sister has left me to do the work by myself? Tell her to help me!"

Life for me has always been filled with responsibilities and stressful demands. Sometimes the demanding pressures of life become so overbearing they are like a yoke of bondage thrown around my neck, home and family responsibilities, work, church, and personal life, not to mention the stresses of societal demands and expectations. We are living in a time and age where things change at a rapid rate. It changes rapidly, and with each change stems forth demands sometimes that are almost impossible to meet. There are demands for cultural and traditional changes. Demands to fashion, home and family improvement. There is information buildup and breakdown, changes in the communication methods, keeping up with technological times, and demands, especially on the job or at school – are some of the catalysts that drive change and can lead to pressure. There is always pressure to learn the new ways of getting new investors or faster ways of getting work done. As Christians, where do we even find time to breathe in all of this?

"Now as they were traveling along, He entered a village; and a woman named Martha welcomed Him into her home. She had a sister called Mary, who was seated at the Lord's feet, listening to His word. But Martha was distracted with all her preparations; and she came up to Him and said,

"Lord, do You not care that my sister has left me to do all the serving alone? Then tell her to help me." But the Lord answered and said to her, "Martha, Martha, you are worried and bothered about so many things; but only one thing is necessary, for Mary has chosen the good part, which shall not be taken away from her" **(Luke 10:38-42** *NASB 1995).*

How often do we labor in that which we deem needful to our betterment of life when the most essential and rewarding peace and rest we can find is at the feet of Jesus? What do we do when the demanding pressures of life come knocking at our door when our mind is overly active, hurling all the things we have not yet accomplished for the day or the week? The call of our hearts is to be still.

Be still and know that I am God **(Psalm 46:10** *KJV).*

"When the oceans rise and thunder roar, I will soar with you above the storm. Father, you are King over the flood, I will be still, and know you are God. Find rest my soul in Christ alone; know his

---

This song speaks to how noisome and crowded life can become, but if we seek God in our quiet times for rest to our troubled souls, we can receive His power that will bring us calm. The changing world and society we live in should not hinder us from choosing the better part as Mary did. We cannot afford to be encumbered about with much that we do not find time to replenish our soul. The truth is life will always be demanding, but our response to its demands does not have to be the same as the world. They get upset and frustrated when things are not done the way they expect them to be done. At other times they drink, and party in celebration of accomplishments attained. They want things done at light speed without the long hour wait, without taking the time to rest or replenish themselves. Beloved, let us be still and allow God to help us deal with the pressures of life.

Call to Action

When the yoke of burden has fastened its hold on you, accept Jesus' invitation today and come to Him. Take a moment, find a place to be quiet in His presence, and ask God to give you rest for your weary soul.

"Are you weary, carrying a heavy burden? Then come to me. I will refresh your life, for I am your

oasis. Simply join your life with mine. Learn my ways and you'll discover that I'm gentle, humble, easy to please. You will find refreshment and rest in me. For all that I require of you will be pleasant and easy to bear" **(Matthew 11:28-30 TPT).**

DAY 4 - THE CALL OF THE FLESH TO LOVE THE WORLD

1 John 2:15-16 KJV

Love not the world, neither the things that are in the world. If any man love the world, the love of the Father is not in him.

For all that is in the world, the lust of the flesh, and the lust of the eyes, and the pride of life, is not of the Father, but is of the world.

There are different things that we believe we need to survive this life, and those very same things are what we will leave here on this earth when we die.

"While we look not at the things which are seen, but at the things which are not seen: for the things which are seen are temporal; but the things which are not seen are eternal (2 Corinthians 4:18 KJV).

What is your heart fixed on? Moreover, on what foundation does it stand? Some people put their trust in the world and the things of this world. They glory in their many accomplishments and material possessions rather than placing their faith in God. As a Christian, I use to desire the things of this world so much. I often longed to be in relationships, work in a fancy job, drive a posh car, buy the finest clothes and shoes, excelling academically. Of course, all this I desired while going to church. It was a crazy time in my life.

I would indulge in pleasures that go against the principles of my very own salvation, and there were days when I would have money enough to flaunt and do whatever I please yet, having indulged in the many things that would appeal to my flesh, I only grew empty and tired. When we fix our hearts on the temporal things that avail to nothing, we erect idols in our lives, which draws us away from God and the things that will benefit God's kingdom, and our lives in the world to come.

"Don't keep hoarding for yourselves earthly treasures that can be stolen by thieves. Material wealth eventually rusts, decays, and loses its value. Instead, stockpile heavenly treasures for yourselves that cannot be stolen and will never rust, decay, or lose their value **(Matthew 6:19-20 TPT).***

For your heart will always pursue what you value as your treasure **(Matthew 6:21 TPT).**

Each day we are reminded of the many deaths worldwide and all their many left behind accomplishments. Some people's achievements and memories are honored from time to time, while others are recognized for a season and then fade away. Beloved,

"Love not the world, neither the things that are in the world. If any man love the world, the love of the Father is not in him. For all that is in the world, the lust of the flesh, and the lust of the eyes, and the pride of life, is not of the Father, but is of the world. And the world passeth away, and the lust thereof: but he that doeth the will of God abideth for ever **(1 John 2:15-17 KVJ).**

It is a shame to think that some Christians are caught up in these kinds of situations, hoarding the goods of this life. They become frivolous in their lifestyles, wanton wasters, idolatrous and greedy. Their hearts are consumed by gluttony and soon dried up because they seek the gifts rather than the giver of the "gifts". The rich young man loved his money more than God in *Matthew 19:16–30*, a fact that Jesus astutely pointed out.

The issue was not that the young man was rich but that he "treasured" his riches and did not "treasure" what he could have in Christ. Jesus told the man to sell his possessions and give to the poor, "and he will have treasure in heaven. Then come, follow me" (verse 21). The young man left Jesus sad because he was wealthy. He chose this world's treasure and did not lay up treasure in heaven. He was unwilling to make Jesus his treasure. The young man was very religious, but Jesus exposed his heart of greed. We are to treasure the Lord Jesus most of all. When Jesus is our treasure, we will commit our resources—our money, time, and talents—to His work in this world. Our motivation for what we do is important **(1 Corinthians 10:31 KJV).** Paul encourages servants that God has an eternal reward for those who are motivated to serve Christ: The Lord will be faithful to reward us for the service we give Him. The treasures that await the child of God will far outweigh any trouble, inconvenience, or persecution we may face **(Romans 8:18).** We can serve the Lord wholeheartedly, knowing that God is the one keeping score, and His reward will be abundantly gracious.

Call to Action

What is it that you so desire in this life, that you put aside God's time to pursue it? STOP! Turn around and seek God's kingdom today. He will grant you according to the desires of your heart. Ask Him to search you now to see what consumes you, if it is the things that pertain to this world or the things concerning His kingdom.

DAY 5 - THE FLAW OF DISHONESTY

Proverbs 12:22 KJV

Lying lips are an abomination to the Lord,

But those who deal faithfully are His delight.

Honesty begins with confession, and sometimes if we wish to confess, some of us struggle with the flaw of dishonesty. What is dishonesty? If you say that a person or their behavior is dishonest, you mean that they are not truthful or sincere and you cannot trust them. That's what men say, but what does God say about dishonesty?

*"There are six things the LORD hates, seven that are detestable to him: haughty eyes, a lying tongue, hands that shed innocent blood, a heart that devises wicked schemes, feet that are quick to rush into evil, a false witness who pours out lies and a person who stirs up conflict in the community. **(Proverbs 6:16-19 NIV)***

For You are not a God who takes pleasure in wickedness; No evil dwells with You.

The boastful shall not stand before Your eyes; You hate all who do iniquity.

*You destroy those who speak falsehood; The Lord abhors the man of bloodshed and deceit. **(Psalm 5:4-6 NASB 1995)***

What need I else to say? The truth is whether Christians or non-Christians, we all should practice being honest. Honesty is a significant character trait that will take us further in life and promote us to where we seek to reach, be it in this world or in the one to come.

"For we aim at what is honorable not only in the Lord's sight but also in the sight of man. (2 Corinthians 8:21 ESV).

An honest person represents himself just as he is and tells others the truth about themselves. Honesty is not "expressing everything that goes through your mind." That is transparency, and a person can be transparent without being honest. However, no one can be consistently honest without a commitment to the truth. At times, honesty will hurt someone's feelings, but that does not mean that dishonesty is preferable. Lying is always reproved in Scripture. God does not accept a person who "practices deceit."

"Whoever desires to love life and see good days, let him keep his tongue from evil and his lips from speaking deceit; let him turn away from evil and do good; let him seek peace and pursue it. For the eyes of the Lord are on the righteous, and his ears are open to their prayer. But the face of the Lord is against those who do evil." (1 Peter 3:10-12 ESV).

I have always tried to make honesty a part of my lifestyle; it is something that I practice every day. At times, I feel tempted to lie whenever I find myself in difficult situations. While at other times, because of the work that I do, I am exposed to large sums of money so I may feel tempted at times to want to take some of it. There are other instances for example, where I may find someone's expensive phone, or their purse, or even if I get more than my change from a taxi driver or after purchasing items at a supermarket that I would feel tempted to deal unfaithfully in these matters. I do not steal and would never steal, but I know that I am not alone; some of us can be identify with these kinds of situations that will cause us to feel tempted. Therefore, *honesty is an intentional lifestyle in which we must choose to be always honest and trustworthy in our dealings with humanity.* I have learned each day that through daily confession and acknowledgment of my frailty to God, He gives me the grace and strength I need to be honest in prayer and in my life.

If you struggle with the flaw of dishonesty, you do not have to feel ashamed. Confide in someone and seek God's help or professional help if you so desire. If everyone in this world should share a flaw of their character, even those we look up to so much, you would then realize that you are not alone, not to mention how surprised you would be to see how skillfully masked some of us are. God loves us so much that He gave the life of His only begotten son for the salvation of the entire world. Not for us to live with the plagues and shortcomings of our lives that hinder us from entirely going forward and embracing our destinies, but that we can find Him to be all that we need and to cast all our cares, flaws, and shortcomings on Him. This enables us to live life in its full abundance and liberty.

Here's a word of advice.

*"Let what you say be 'Yes' or 'No'; anything more than this comes from evil. **(Matthew 5:37 KJV).***

*"For by thy words thou shalt be justified, and by thy words thou shalt be condemned. **(Matthew 12:37 KJV).***

When we understand the importance of our words and how we should speak, guided by God's word, we can make the right declarations that will bring about Salvation.

*"For with the heart man believeth unto righteousness; and with the mouth confession is made unto salvation. **(Romans 10:10 KJV)***

Now it behooves us as children of the Most High God to understand our position in Christ.

*For ye are dead, and your life is hid with Christ in God **(Colossians 3:3 KJV).***

Seeing this, we should therefore seek to be imitators of that which is good as the scripture says,

"Therefore be imitators of God as dear children (Ephesians 5:1 NKJV).

When we do this, our whole life will change. We will reshape our personality as well as our speech, behaviors, and attitudes towards life.

Finally, brothers, whatever is true, whatever is honorable, whatever is just, whatever is pure, whatever is lovely, whatever is commendable, if there is any excellence, if there is anything worthy of praise, think about these things. What you have learned and received and heard and seen in me—practice these things, and the God of peace will be with you. (Philippians 4:8-9ESV)

Call to Action

Starting today, the next time you go to pray, tell God something that has been weighing heavily on your heart that you were afraid to say to Him or anyone. When you do this, it will make you feel lighter. Believe that He hears, and He cares enough to help you to handle that situation.

DAY 6 - OPPOSITION

> **Matthew 10:34-40 KJV**
>
> Think not that I am come to send peace on earth: I came not to send peace, but a sword. For I am come to set a man at variance against his father, and the daughter against her mother, and the daughter in law against her mother in law. And a man's foes shall be they of his own household.

It is hard to freely live your life when all you seem to face each day is opposition. The most hurtful opposition one can face comes from those closest to you, and that is your family. All the negativity hurled at you which comes from those who are supposed to understand you, and see where you are coming from, gets the best of you that it hurts you to the point of resentment, tempting you to speak ill of them. Often, I fall prey to this kind of behavior because I get so upset with my family members. I have always had this struggle, and God had to intervene, or else I would have lost my way. Just like every Christian who lives in a home filled with non-Christians, the famous talk hits you whenever you slip or mess up, "Aren't you the one who is a Christian?" If you have not experienced this well, give thanks, but for those who have and still are going through this, let me tell you that God sees, cares, and understand.

Facing opposition is a part of our journey. As Christians, it is one of the world's greatest weapons used against God's people. It is just a shame that even our families put us through such hurtful experiences. They should be the ones to accept us and try to understand the changes that we make or are trying to make to better ourselves. Families should be supportive and seek to understand the directions we choose to take and offer guidance if they believe we are going down the wrong path. You see, Jesus was not exempt, neither are we. He, too, faced opposition from His own family and community in which He grew up.

When Jesus had finished telling these stories and illustrations, he left that part of the country. He returned to Nazareth, his hometown. When he taught there in the synagogue, everyone was amazed and said, "Where does he get this wisdom and the power to do miracles?" Then they scoffed, "He's just the carpenter's son, and we know Mary, his mother, and his brothers—James, Joseph, Simon, and Judas. All his sisters live right here among us. Where did he learn all these things?" And they were deeply offended and refused to believe in him. Then Jesus told them, "A prophet is honored everywhere except in his own hometown and among his own family." And so he did only a few miracles there because of their unbelief **(Matthew 13:53-58 NIV).**

Do you see how powerfully crippling opposition can be, especially from people and family members? Because of their unbelief, Jesus was unable to perform miracles, and I know that many people in Nazareth were sick and in need of healing. As long as you are in this world, you will face opposition. Jesus said,

"If you belonged to the world, it would love you as its own. As it is, you do not belong to the world, but I have chosen you out of the world. That is why the world hates you. You will be hated by everyone because of me, but the one who stands firm to the end will be saved **(John 15:19 NIV).**

Stand firm on the foundation of God; know that He has overcome the world and all that is in the world and life to come so we can trust that He will take us through our times of opposition.

"I have told you these things, so that in me you may have peace. In this world you will have trouble. But take heart! I have overcome the world."(John 16:33 NIV).

Call to Action

If you are facing opposition from anyone, do not get discouraged. Pray for those with whom you face opposition and watch God turn them around through your persistent, faith-filled prayer.

DAY 7 - THE DISEASE OF COMPARISON

2 Corinthians 10:12 NIV

We do not dare to classify or compare ourselves with some who commend themselves. When they measure themselves by themselves and compare themselves with themselves, they are not wise.

All my life, I have struggled with the severe disease of comparison. It made my life an experience of hell on earth. I lived in torment, with ferocious anger, and resentment towards my life. I spent most of my time complaining rather than giving God thanks for the many blessings that I received from Him day by day. Of course, I was unable to see all that God was doing for me because not only was I blinded by my ungratefulness, but my envy for the success of others also blinded me. The blessings I thought I was to receive and the things I thought would make my life better, I did not get them, but I certainly saw others receiving them. Obviously, this is not a way for anyone to live, and throughout my life, I have come to learn that. Sometimes we play the unfair game of comparison, yet no one ever wins at the end of it. The game of comparison was never designed in the first place to crown winners. We compare ourselves to others regarding our intelligence, academics, godliness, parenting styles, body image, success, marital status, fashion abilities, wealth, how crafty we are, how disciplined we are, how much we can fit on our plate, etc.

Comparison is an enemy that causes destruction and it is the thief of joy. Comparison goes hand in hand with envy, low self-confidence, depression, idolatry, greed, grudge, covetousness, hatred, evil imagination, ill-will, mean-spirited competitiveness, jealousy, lust, a compromise of our ability to trust others as well as death. *Yes! You heard right, death.* Listen! God never made a mistake when He created you. The very fact that you look, shape, speak, and walk the way you do is because the master sculpture made you and was pleased with His work. Then God said,

> *"Let Us make man in Our image, according to Our likeness; So God created man in his [own] image, in the image of God created he him; male and female created he them* **(Genesis 1:26-27 KJV).**

> *"It is I who made the earth, and created man upon it. I stretched out the heavens with My hands And I ordained all their host.* **(Isaiah 45:12 NASB 1995)**

There can only be the one you with the set appropriate personality, uniqueness, skills, talent, and abilities. Understanding who you are plays a vital role in this life as it guides us to live confident, wholesome, purposeful, and directed lives.

"Comparison is the thief of joy."

- Theodore Roosevelt

When we compare ourselves to others, we rob ourselves of the deposited inheritance of unending joy that salvation brings.

God is a God of variety, and His handiwork is seen throughout the entire world. When we see the multiplicity of His creation and humanity, they all come in different shapes, sizes, colors, and language, distinguishing elements of His creative artistic abilities.

*"Thus says God the Lord, Who created the heavens and stretched them out, Who spread out the earth and its offspring, Who gives breath to the people on it And spirit to those who walk in it. **(Isaiah 42:5 BSB)***

An excerpt from https://www.christianity.com/christian-life/spiritual-growth/the-comparison-game.html states:

"Comparison reveals our brokenness. We compare ourselves because deep inside, we are dissatisfied with what we have and who we are.

Whether we feel good or bad after we compare ourselves to someone else, we do it because things are not right inside of us. It is a heart issue. Comparison is a poisonous fruit of discontentment, which admits that we are not satisfied with how

God made us, that we are not happy with where He has placed us, and that we do not appreciate the life He has ordained for us. Comparing ourselves to others is an insult to God.

"Not that we dare to classify or compare ourselves with some of those who are commending themselves. But when they measure themselves by one another and compare themselves with one another, they are without understanding (2 Corinthians 10:12 ESV).

While comparing ourselves to others may distract us from the real issues in our hearts, it does not heal those issues or deal with our sins. The only way we can break free of this comparison trap is by finding our hope and identity in Christ.

https://www.christianity.com/christian-life/spiritual-growth/the-comparison-game.html

Call to Action

When you wake up, write down one thing you are grateful for and one thing you admire about yourself. Do this every day, and you will be amazed at how happy you begin to feel when you spend the time to honestly give thanks for what you have and who you are.

DAY 8 - THE POWER OF SUFFERING

Philippians 3:10 KJV

That I may know him, and the power of his resurrection, and the fellowship of his sufferings, being made conformable unto his death;

Ever so often, we underestimate the power of suffering. If we dare to be honest, this is one part of our journey we all wish we would never have to go through. Nevertheless, as long as God calls us, we all MUST travel this road.

> *"Then Jesus said to his disciples, If any of you wants to be my follower, you must give up your own way, take up your cross, and follow me* **(Matthew 16:24 NLT).**

These were the words spoken by Jesus to His disciples, and today we are disciples of Jesus, so this, therefore, applies to us. I doubt we will ever come across anything that Jesus instructs us to do that He has not done throughout the scriptures. Jesus is the personified embodiment of what suffering entails and the rewards it yields at the end thereof.

> *"Who has believed what he has heard from us? And to whom has the arm of the lord been revealed? For he grew up before him like a young plant, and like a root out of dry ground; he had no form or majesty that we should look at him, and no beauty that we should desire him. He was despised and rejected by men; a man of sorrows, and acquainted with grief;*

and as one from whom men hide their faces he was despised, and we esteemed him not. Surely he has borne our griefs and carried our sorrows; yet we esteemed him stricken, smitten by God, and afflicted. But he was wounded for our transgressions; he was crushed for our iniquities; upon him was the chastisement that brought us peace, and with his stripes we are healed **(Isaiah 53:1-5 ESV).**

For Christ also suffered once for sins, the righteous for the unrighteous, that he might bring us to God, being put to death in the flesh but made alive in the spirit **(1 Peter 3:18 ESV).**

We can share numerous examples regarding the suffering of our Lord Jesus Christ. He never placed Himself on a pedestal as being too good enough to suffer,

"...but emptied himself by taking the form of a servant, being born in the likeness of men. And being found in human form, he humbled himself by becoming obedient to the point of death, even death on a cross." **(Philippians 2:7 ESV).**

If Jesus carried His cross, what would exempt us from following such a momentous radical example? The power that lies within suffering is far beyond our finite understanding. Still, if we try to take a more positive, accepting approach, we can reap substantial eternal rewards that money cannot buy. According to **gotquestions.org/Bible-suffering:**

Christ suffered for the sake of rebuilding a broken relationship gone bad from the beginning of time where man had sinned against God. When Adam sinned, the entire world was affected. Sin entered human experience, and death was the result and so death followed this sin, casting its shadow over all humanity, because all have sinned. God made Him who had no sin to be sin for us, so that in Him we might become the righteousness of God. Christ benefited from becoming the ultimate sacrifice in that: after His resurrection He was glorified, all power was given unto Him, He is seated at the right hand of God with power, He is our only way to the father, salvation and eternal life.

He is our advocate and mediator, He has made one with us in spirit as He now serves as the high priest who can be touched with the feeling of our infirmities, and He was triumphant over the devil and currently holds the keys of death and hell to name a few. It can be very daunting at times, the troubles we feel, the situations we face, and the sufferings we have to endure, but Peter reminded us that

*"Since therefore Christ suffered in the flesh, arm yourselves with the same way of thinking, for whoever has suffered in the flesh has ceased from sin **(1 Peter 4:1 ESV).***

Having a made-up mind to deny ourselves, take up our cross, and endure hardship as a good soldier will allow us to face our sufferings differently with a more positive outlook than to think God is out to get us or He does not care for us at all. When we are experiencing seasons of suffering, the best way to respond and overcome is to draw back on the Word, which provides us with all the answers we need. Some of these truths are;

*"Trust in the Lord with all thine heart; and lean not unto thine own understanding. In all thy ways acknowledge him, and he shall direct thy paths. **(Proverbs 3:5-6 KJV)***

*Rejoice evermore. Pray without ceasing. In everything give thanks: for this is the will of God in Christ Jesus concerning you. **(1 Thessalonians 5:16-18 KJV),***

Like David, encourage yourself in the Lord. When we become more accepting of our sufferings as Christ was, our rewards will be far worth it in the end. When we glory in our sufferings it *called according to his purpose (Romans 8:28 NIV).*

I hope you will be inspired today to change your outlook on your sufferings as the truth, which lies in God, empowers us to be more victorious in the end.

Call to Action

Change your response to your sufferings. Please get in the Word and read what it says regarding your present circumstances. Read it aloud, let it saturate the atmosphere, and increase your faith. Remember,

...faith comes by hearing and hearing the word of God. (Romans 10:17 KJV)

DAY 9 - THE POWER OF THE SPOKEN WORD

Ezekiel 12:25 ESV

For I the Lord will speak, and whatever word I speak will be performed. It will no longer be delayed, for in your days, O rebellious house, I will speak the word and perform it," declares the Lord God."'

The only thing that can withstand hard times is the Word of God. All we need to get through our tough, disappointing, hurtful, confusing times is a word from the Lord.

> *"For the word of God is living and active, sharper than any two-edged sword, piercing to the division of soul and of spirit, of joints and of marrow, and discerning the thoughts and intentions of the **heart** (Hebrews 4:12 ESV).***

When God speaks a word amid our situation, He declares:

> *...it shall not return unto Him void, but it shall accomplish that which He pleases, and it shall prosper in the thing whereto He sent it **(Isaiah 55:11 KJV).***

> *And the same day, when the even was come, he saith unto them, Let us pass over unto the other side. And when they had sent away the multitude, they took him even as he was in the ship. And there were also with him other little ships. And there arose a great storm of wind, and the waves beat into the ship, so that it was now full. And he was in*

*the hinder part of the ship, asleep on a pillow: and
they awake him, and say unto him, Master, carest
thou not that we perish? And he arose, and rebuked
the wind, and said unto the sea, Peace, be still. And
the wind ceased, and there was a great calm And
he said unto them, Why are ye so fearful? how is it
that ye have no faith? And they feared exceedingly,
and said one to another, What manner of man is
this, that even the wind and the sea obey him?*
(Mark 4:35-41 KJV.)

When we speak the Word of God, it cancels all doubts and
fears or whatever uncertainties that lie within our hearts. Remember
Jairus, who had a daughter that was sick? He requested healing for
her from Jesus, and this is what transpired;

*"While Jesus was still speaking, some people came
from the house of Jairus, the synagogue leader.
"Your daughter is dead," they said. "Why bother
the teacher anymore?" Overhearing what they
said, Jesus told him, "Don't be afraid; just believe"*
(Matthew 5:35-36 NIV).

This scenario is a perfect example highlighting when the Lord
speaks amidst what seems to be a hopeless situation. When the
servants of Jairus told him that his daughter had died, Jesus knew
within Himself that Jairus would start to doubt because he had seemed

to reach a roadblock. However, Jesus quickly reassured him with His Word, not to be afraid but believe, and the comforting words of Jesus prospered and were not returned unto Him void. There are many accounts of the authoritative transcendent power found in the spoken Word of God. Jesus spoke to the wind, and it obeyed Him. He spoke to Elijah when He felt afraid and suicidal, and Elijah regained strength to continue on his journey.

He prayed the word and multitudes were fed, He spoke the Word while He was tempted and overcame the devil, Jesus commanded devils to flee, and they were cast out. He spoke to the fig tree, and it dried up. He spoke to the fish, which brought Jonah to his commissioned journey. We can trust that when God speaks, something will happen,

...for Man shall not live by bread alone, but by every word that proceedeth out of the mouth of God (Matthew 4:4 KJV).

I can recall the many times I had to seek God for a word while going through difficult periods in my life. What has helped me throughout my walk with God is the Word of God. I recall one particular morning I got up to pray; worry consumed me as I began to think about my life, I couldn't focus on prayer, and that's when God said to me, "seek ye first the kingdom of God and His righteousness".

Friends, I was rebuked. I immediately reached out to God for His forgiveness, and He later went on to confirm that same word throughout the day. There were many times when I was troubled in my mind, and sleep went from me during the night seasons. Jesus never failed to speak words of comfort to me when I took up the bible to read. When God speaks the word amid our situations, there is a powerful reaction in the spirit realm. Though we may not see it with our natural eyes, the spirit gives life; the flesh profits nothing. The words that He speaks to us are spirit, and they are life *(John 6:63 NKJV)*. God talks to us in many ways. Through prayer, the scriptures, the Holy Spirit, the church, people, His creation, our situations, dreams, visions, etc., no matter God's way of speaking to us, we can be sure that His Word will make a difference in our lives.

Call to Action

Let us be still in our difficult times and listen for God to speak.

> *For faith comes from hearing, and hearing by the word of God (Romans 10:17 KJV).*

Moreover, when we believe that God has spoken by faith, we can conclude that it is well done. Like

> *"Ezra who blessed the LORD, the great God. And all the people answered, Amen, Amen, with lifting up their hands: and they bowed their heads, and*

worshipped the LORD with their faces to the ground (Nehemiah 8:6 KJV).

He who has promised is faithful even unto the very end.

DAY 10 - TEARS ARE A LANGUAGE THAT GOD UNDERSTANDS

Psalms 31:9 KJV

Have mercy upon me, O Lord, for I am in trouble: mine eye is consumed with grief, yea, my soul and my belly.

I think I cry more than I speak. I feel a level of connection when I pour out my heart crying to God in prayer. There are days I am left to handle the excruciating effects of this world's sting through the many painful setbacks, disagreements, conflicts, and trouble that befall me. The only real place of comfort and assurance for me is when I bow my face to the ground lamenting before the only one who seems to understand. Sometimes all you have to do, all you can do is to lift your hands to heaven amid your pain and cry. What better language is there than the very drop of our tears? Every single tear carries its own weight of speech that reaches the heart of the greatest linguist.

"Often you wonder why tears come into your eyes and burdens seem to be much more than you can stand. But God is standing near He sees your falling tears and tears are a language that God understands." **Tears Are A Language – Heritage Singers**

Hannah was in distress. Because of her barrenness, she was desperate to give her husband an heir.

When words failed her each time she prayed, she cried unto the Lord speaking with a language only desperate times understood, tears.

> *"So Hannah rose up after they had eaten in Shiloh, and after they had drunk. Now Eli the priest sat upon a seat by a post of the temple of the Lord. And she was in bitterness of soul, and prayed unto the Lord, and wept sore. And she vowed a vow, and said, O Lord of hosts, if thou wilt indeed look on the affliction of thine handmaid, and remember me, and not forget thine handmaid, but wilt give unto thine handmaid a man child, then I will give him unto the Lord all the days of his life, and there shall no razor come upon his head. And it came to pass, as she continued praying before the Lord, that Eli marked her mouth. Now Hannah, she spake in her heart; only her lips moved, but her voice was not heard: therefore Eli thought she had been drunken. And Eli said unto her, How long wilt thou be drunken? Put away thy wine from thee. And Hannah answered and said, No, my Lord, I am a woman of a sorrowful spirit: I have drunk neither wine nor strong drink, but have poured out my soul before the Lord. (1 Samuel 1:9-10 KJV)*

Often, we experience pressing situations that cost us our ability to speak (not literally) but in a way that allows us to be unable to express the severity of the discomfort we feel. Hanna suffered greatly. Her soul was in distress. Her demonstration of desperation drove her to tears, but God came through for her in the end.

Call to Action

Today if you are too overwhelmed to pray, if words fail you, still talk to God, weep, prostrate, express yourself to Him in prayer; He sees your tears He understands what you are going through. His words declare:

"You have kept count of my tossings; put my tears in your bottle. Are they not in your book? **(Psalm 56:8 ESV)**

"Lord, you know all my desires and deepest longings. My tears are liquid words and you can read them all." **(Psalm 38:9 TPT).**

He will one day wipe away all tears from our eyes.

DAY 11 - MY SCARS MAKE ME BEAUTIFUL

Galatians 6:17 ESV

From now on let no one cause me trouble, for I bear on my body the marks of Jesus.

The scars we receive are not very bad as we thought. Some serve as reminders of our mistakes, joys, sorrows, adversities, adventures, addictions, journeying, and fear. The scars we receive from the above-mentioned can change our appearance, perspective, mindset, and lives forever. They can also alter how we feel about ourselves, how we deal with situations, and how we treat people. Each time we find ourselves in a particular situation that reunites us with those memories of our scars; we often are washed with the feeling of regret or happiness. We may question why we put ourselves in such a position in the first place depending on how the scars came about.

If a child got hurt while riding their bike in a particular area of their home, and the incident has left a scar, each time that child revisits that same area where they incurred the injury; it will bring back the memory of how it all happened. But such memory will serve as a lesson and, the child will now take a different approach when he/she goes to ride the bike in that area so that the past would not repeat itself thus, preventing him/her from incurring another injury. We must always seek to learn from the incidents where we have suffered our scars and try to be better by moving on from such situations.

Many people today have suffered and still suffer from hurtful experiences that have caused and are causing scars in their lives. I can personally attest to this. There are times when I give myself over into thinking that if an operation were to be conducted on my heart, it would reveal how badly damaged it is, as it is the place where I have suffered scars beyond measure. Scars can be emotional, physical, mental, verbal, and even spiritual. However, no matter the scar, there has to be a way provided for us to bounce back from such situations and an effective mechanism put in place for us to overcome. The death of Jesus is authenticated and evidenced by the scars He received when He was crucified at Calvary. He was nailed to the cross and pierced in His side. **(John 20:24-29 NIV).** Jesus was also left with scars that He received after He was beaten **(John 19:1 KJV)**. Both of these events which led to Jesus' triumphant victory over sin, death, hell and the grave serves as the indelible mark that is imprinted upon us when we exercise faith in Him and accept Him as our Lord and savior. Physical marks over time tend to fade or be replaced by our skin. Conversely, the mark printed in our souls distinguishes us and remains forever.

> *From henceforth let no man trouble me: for I bear in my body the marks of the Lord Jesus (Galatians 6:17 KJV). But he was wounded for our transgressions, he was bruised for our iniquities: the chastisement of our peace was upon him; and with his stripes we are healed **(Isaiah 53:5 KJV)**.*

Beloved, remember that our wounds are not forever. It will heal after a while, and depending on the severity of our wounds, it may or may not leave a scar. However, if a scar is left because of its severity, let us embrace it with much positivity. Our scars do not have to be painful reminders; they can be beautiful birthmarks of victory. Amen.

Call to Action

Love every part of your journey. If you get a few bruises or cuts along the way, do not quickly write them off as something terrible. Everything you go through and experience along this Christian journey is useful to God, the master quilt builder. Some persons build quilts from different patches of materials that usually hold a particular memory. That is what God is doing in your life. Every patch of your life is being sewed together to make a beautifully quilted story.

DAY 12 - CLOSED DOOR OF OPPORTUNITY

Psalm 84:11 KJV

For the LORD God is a sun and shield: the LORD will give grace and glory: no good thing will he withhold from them that walk uprightly.

Sometimes we have to experience closed doors of opportunities for us to realize that not all is lost. We pray for opportunities, and when they are given to us sometimes, it doesn't match our true potential as individuals, or it takes away so much of our time that we no longer get to do the things that aid in the growth of our lives spiritually. God will never deny anyone a chance at living life in abundance; His wish is

> *"...above all things that we may prosper and be in health, even as our soul prospereth* **(3 John 1:2 KJV).**

> *No good thing will he withhold from them that walk uprightly* **(Psalm 84:11 KJV).**

Many opportunities will come our way, but I can safely say that not all of them are worth taking. When we are provided with various opportunities, it is critical to seek God's will because not all of them represent God's planned will for our lives. If we do His will and are faithful, all the opportunities we seek, as long as they are a part of His good plan for our lives, He will give them.

There will come a time that, even against our wish, He will open a particular door of opportunity that we may not be qualified to handle. However, if we trust Him to go through with His plans, He will do the impossible to make us qualified in such a situation. David's father and brothers never considered him fit or qualified to be king, yet he was the one whom God had chosen out of all his brothers. In the eyes of their father and Samuel, they looked the part of being anointed as king but God chose David because

"the LORD seeth not as man seeth; for man looketh on the outward appearance, but the LORD looketh on the heart (1 Samuel 16:7 KJV).

We quickly become excited about new opportunities, especially if they promote prosperity. Who would not be happy about the slightest chance to better their lives? Here is where the problem lies. Not because it appears to be a good opportunity means that it is God's will or His intended way of blessing us. While living a humble life as a shepherd boy, David undoubtedly devoted his life to God in service, even though the job he held was considered one of the lowest positions of his time anyone could have. His heart was right before God, and as such, the Lord saw it fit to anoint him as the next king over His people Israel.

We seek opportunities and fail to receive them because God sees our hearts and knows what is best for us. What we think is a chance for prosperity could also be a setup for failure and the loss of everything that we already have. If you seek opportunities for the betterment of your life, you cannot go wrong if you

"Trust in the Lord with all thine heart; and lean not unto your own understanding. In all your ways acknowledge him, and he shall direct your paths ***(Proverbs 3:5-6 KJV).***

Call to Action

Practice to become more prudent in your dealings when you seek to go forward in life. Be more willing to seek God first before you accept the opportunities offered to you. Seek God's desired will for your life, and you will never go wrong.

DAY 13 - THE HAUNTING GUILT OF OUR PAST

> **Romans 8:1-2 TPT**
>
> Beloved there remains no accusing voice of condemnation against those who are joined in life-union with Jesus, the Anointed One. For the "law" of the Spirit of life flowing through the anointing of Jesus has liberated us from the "law" of sin and death.

As children of God, sometimes we find ourselves on a roller coaster of being haunted by our past, and being plagued day in and day out, night after night. There are times we become overwhelmed by the feeling of guilt that we allow ourselves to believe the lies of the devil. I was in this position, and I know this feeling all too well. Once, I thought I would never be free from the noisome accusations that repeatedly pound the walls of my mind regarding the sins from my past. It was a horrible experience, which clouded my judgment about people, God, and most importantly, me.

Even after being saved, it was intensified to the point where I heard voices in my head screaming; "I will never be enough. That God's grace cannot be enough to save me, God doesn't love me, I will never amount to anything, and I am ugly and unattractive". I cried myself to sleep many nights and I faced depression often because I could not seem to properly deal with my situation.

However after a while, I began to realize that the only way to combat the attacks of the enemy, the accuser of the brethren *(Revelation 12:10 KJV)* was to be more involved with God's Word by studying, meditating, journaling and praying God's truth openly about me. As newborn babes it is of utmost importance that we are fed with the sincere milk of the Word; to enable our growth *(1 Peter*

2:2 KJV). We cannot allow our past to condemn us, torment us, define us, inflict us, dictate to us, or imprint its disease-ridden lies upon us. We are told in scriptures that:

*"we are buried with him (Christ) by baptism into death: that like as Christ was raised up from the dead by the glory of the Father, even so we also should walk in newness of life **(Romans 6:4 KJV)**.*

*If any man be in Christ, he is a new creature: old things are passed away; behold, all things are become new **(2 Corinthians 5:17 KJV)**.*

*Knowing this, that our old man is crucified with him, that the body of sin might be destroyed, that henceforth we should not serve sin. For he that is dead is freed from sin **(Romans 6:6 KJV)**.*

Can you believe this truth? Yes! Yes, we can because this is the inspired word of God. Because of Jesus' sacrifice and His Word spoken before time concerning us, we who have accepted Him as our Lord and Savior, who reigns this day in our hearts by faith, no longer have to believe the lies of a defeated foe whose intent is to kill, steal and destroy *(John 10:10 KJV)*. There is no need for us to feel worn out by our past mistakes and actions. Each day we experience the mercies of the Lord, which are new every morning. No longer do we serve sin,

"For by one offering he hath perfected forever them that are sanctified. Whereof the Holy Ghost also is a witness to us: for after that he had said before, This is the covenant that I will make with them after those days, saith the Lord, I will put my laws into their hearts, and in their minds will I write them; And their sins and iniquities will I remember no more. Now where remission of these is, there is no more offering for sin. Having therefore, brethren, boldness to enter into the holiest by the blood of Jesus, By a new and living way, which he hath consecrated for us, through the veil, that is to say, his flesh; And having an high priest over the house of God; Let us draw near with a true heart in full assurance of faith, having our hearts sprinkled from an evil conscience, and our bodies washed with pure water **(Hebrews 10:14-22 KJV).***

Call to Action

To live free from the haunting guilt of our past is an intentional step we must take every day. Everyone, at some point in their lives where tempted and accused by the devil, and the reason they are alive today is that they chose not to allow their past to dictate their outcome. You are free; the Word of God explicitly declares that truth.

When the haunting guilt of your past comes back to haunt you, make that intentional step, tell the devil that Christ has set you free from the condemning thoughts and actions of your past. You are no longer a slave to fear.

DAY 14 - THE HOARDERS OF THIS LIFE

Colossians 3:1 KJV

If ye then be risen with Christ, seek those things which are above, where Christ sitteth on the right hand of God.

Ever so often, we become hoarders, collectors of the things of this world. We place our trust and hope in them with our minds and affection affixed on temporal things; things of no real value that only sparks pleasure for a season. Nothing lasts forever; Job said it,

*"naked I came from my mother's womb, And naked shall I return there **(Job 1:21 KJV)**.*

A timely reminder of this was illustrated in ***Luke 12:16-21***.

"Jesus then gave them this illustration: "A wealthy land owner had a farm that produced bumper crops. In fact, it filled his barns to overflowing! He thought, 'What should I do now that every barn is full and I have nowhere else to store more? I know what I'll do! I'll tear down the barns and build one massive barn that will hold all my grain and goods. Then I can just sit back, surrounded with comfort and ease. I'll enjoy life with no worries at all.'
"God said to him, 'What a fool you are to trust in your riches and not in me. This very night the messengers of death are demanding to take your life. Then who will get all the wealth you have stored up for yourself?' This is what will happen to

all those who fill up their lives with everything but
God." (TPT)

"A man's life consisteth not in the abundance of the
things which he possesseth (Luke 12:15 KJV).

As children of God, we are no longer a part of this world. We are now sojourners occupying until our appointed time of Jesus' return. We once walked after the course of this world. We longed after and partook of all the things that this world has to offer. Now we have been redeemed, given a new mind, and a new nature.

"If ye then be risen with Christ, seek those things
which are above, where Christ sitteth on the right
hand of God. (Colossians 3:1-2 KJV)

. For where our treasure is, there will our hearts be
also (Matthew 6:21 KJV).

We should build our hope on things eternal. If we want to be hoarders, then hoard the things that will aid us in the life to come. For Christ, stockpile souls and be hoarders of love, compassion, and peace, spreading the gospel's good news to everyone we meet. One day all the temporal things will pass away, and you will go to your grave without them. My mentor always told me only what we do for Christ will last.

Call to Action

When last have you searched your treasure chest to see what you have been storing? The treasure chest I speak of is your heart. Always remember what comes out of the mouth proceeds from the heart, and this defiles a person.

For out of the heart come evil thoughts, murder, adultery, sexual immorality, theft, false witness, slander. (Matthew 15:18-19 ESV).

Ask the Lord to Search you, and know your heart:

- Try you.
- Know your thoughts: And see if *there be any* wicked way in you.
- Lead you in the way everlasting. *(Psalm 139:23-24 KJV)*

DAY 15 - FIRST CLASS HONORS DEGREE IN THE FIELD OF JUDGMENTALISM

John 7:24 KJV

Judge not according to the appearance, but judge righteous judgment

Most of us are awarded with first class honors degrees in the field of judgmentalism. We are experts at making judgments about others as opposed to ourselves.

> *"Do not judge others, and you will not be judged. For you will be treated as you treat others. The standard you use in judging is the standard by which you will be judged (**Matthew 7:1-2 NLT**).*

The language that God speaks is the language of love. As long as we are called by His name, our language should also be that of love. God never seeks to believe the worst of anyone, no matter if their sins or lifestyle choices say otherwise. He gives them the opportunity through His love to become better by helping them in their areas of weakness, and that is the example we should follow at all times. Jesus never judged the thief on the cross, the prodigal son, the woman caught in adultery, Peter who denied him, Mary Magdalene, and the many others who lived contrary to his will. Their lifestyle condemned them, yet Christ never cast a word, eye, or action of judgment against them; instead, He lovingly embraced them, exhorting them to sin no more.

I can recall many times in my life where I resorted to being judgmental. I would look at persons and just by one thing that they did, I would formulate an opinion in my mind of them, and until they could prove me wrong that what I thought of them was not true, they would forever be what I thought of them even if my assumption were wrong all together. I judged persons based on the size of their sins as opposed to my sins. At one point in my life my prayers were like the Pharisee in **Luke 18:11-12** which says,

> *The Pharisee stood and prayed thus with himself, God, I thank thee, that I am not as other men are, extortioners, unjust, adulterers, or even as this publican. I fast twice in the week, I give tithes of all that I possess. (KJV)*

Even though it was not in so many words as the scripture states, I had that kind of attitude in prayer. I would pray and tell God all the good things I think He wanted to hear while pointing out that I did not sin as big this week like *Sister Plantain* or *Brother Pan* did.

Eventually, I had to get rid of that mentality, not that it was an easy thing to do; because when you have lived a particular way for a while your belief generally governs your action. Nevertheless, through much prayer, crying, pleading to God about my disease-ridden ways I gradually got the healing I deserved through the Word of God and through His overflowing grace, mercy and love for me. We are so undeserving; all of us have had the privilege of being saved by grace through faith. Our lifestyle explicitly declared us guilty before God, but He chose to

*"blotteth out our transgressions for his own sake, and will not remember our sins **(Isaiah 43:25 KJV).***

*God said for I will be merciful to their unrighteousness, and their sins and their iniquities will I remember no more **(Hebrews 8:12 KJV).***

We have no right to judge others because we are in no way better. If God accepted us and spoke the language of love over us, let us follow His example and do the same towards our brothers and sisters.

*The Lord sees not as man sees: man looks on the outward appearance, but the Lord looks on the heart." **(1 Samuel 16:7 ESV).***

Call to Action

In the sight of God, we are one, and if we paused long enough to see through the eyes of God, we would treat and understand each other better. There will be no room to judge. Each time you feel tempted to judge someone, make a cynical remark about something, or even if you see a person at a particular place, or hear something about someone without the full story before you say anything, stop, and look at your life. Think back on all the times you might have been in the same position as the person you intend to judge and remember how God was merciful to you. Extend that same hand of mercy to that person. Do not indulge in conversations about others or comment in that conversation without knowing the full story.

DAY 16 - WHAT PATH WILL YOU TAKE IN THIS JOURNEY OF LIFE?

Psalms 32:8 KJV

I will instruct thee and teach thee in the way which thou shalt go: I will guide thee with mine eye.

Life will take us on a journey. Where it may lead us, only time and the decisions that we make will tell.

> *"Today I have given you the choice between life and death, between blessings and curses. Now I call on heaven and earth to witness the choice you make. Oh, that you would choose life, so that you and your descendants might live!* **(Deuteronomy30:19 NLT)**

> *"Enter through the narrow gate. For wide is the gate and broad and easy to travel is the path that leads the way to destruction and eternal loss, and there are many who enter through it. But small is the gate and narrow and difficult to travel is the path that leads the way to [everlasting] life, and there are few who find it* **(Matthew 7:13-14 AMP).**

What decisions are we making today that will lead us through the narrow gate? The road to mass destruction is so easy to trod, but never can we endure to walk the path that presents us victorious and more than conquerors at the end. Life continually throws us reminders. It points us to all our flaws and miscalculations of our intended directions. When we seek to walk in our way as Christians, rarely do we ever achieve what we set out to accomplish. Why?

> *"Because the way of man is not in himself: it is not in man that walketh to direct his steps* ***(Jeremiah 10:23 KJV).***

When we choose to follow Christ, we choose to abandon our knowledge, thoughts, and way of life, everything that pertains to us. The cross of Jesus Christ is one that signifies self-denial. It was the cross that led to our salvation, so this means we no longer control our lives.

> *"Then said Jesus unto his disciples, If any man will come after me, let him deny himself, and take up his cross, and follow me. For whosoever will save his life shall lose it: and whosoever will lose his life for my sake shall find it* ***(Matthew 16:24-26 KJV).***

Jesus can be in total control of our lives if we allow Him to. It behooves us to trust Him with every single detail of our life because the choices that we make in life will affect us whether we choose, good or bad.

We have been given the perfect opportunity to choose between life and death, freedom and bondage. Never are we pressured or forced by God to choose the path that leads to salvation. He freely gives the invitation to all. It is now on us whether we want to accept it or not. Nevertheless, He offers His advice of wisdom, and He says choose life.

None of us knows what life has to offer. It is unpredictable, but not to God; He is omniscient. He knows everything and exercises control and supremacy over all things. That is why we live by faith and trust in the one who holds tomorrow.

"many things about tomorrow, I don't seem to understand. But I know who holds tomorrow and I know He holds my hand." – **I Know Who Holds Tomorrow (*Songwriter - Ira Stanphill*)**

*"For I know the thoughts that I think toward you, saith the LORD, thoughts of peace, and not of evil, to give you an expected end. (**Jeremiah 29:11 KJV**)*

Call to Action

Instead of going about life your own way, planning your course, becoming frustrated and upset time after time when things do not work out the way you planned, why not turn it over to Jesus? He knows the way that you should take and the outcome of it. Pray a prayer of total surrender today and ask the Lord to take full control of your life and lead you into the right path to take.

DAY 17 - ENDURANCE IN TIMES OF ADVERSITY

James 1:12 AMPC

Blessed [happy, spiritually prosperous, favored by God] is the man who is steadfast under trial and perseveres when tempted; for when he has passed the test and been approved, he will receive the [victor's] crown of life which the Lord has promised to those who love Him.

Because of the intensity of our adversities, over time our faith comes under pressure by our doubts and questions of unbelief, much like whether God will deliver us. In our times of pressing, we say, "Lord, I am not sure how long I will be able to bear this test." The truth is, if this is what we say and how we think, then our means by which we were able to endure was never reliance on God but ourselves.

*"Come unto me, all ye that labour and are heavy laden, and I will give you rest. Take my yoke upon you, and learn of me; for I am meek and lowly in heart: and ye shall find rest unto your souls. For my yoke is easy, and my burden is light (**Matthew 11:28-30 KJV**).*

When God is doing a work in us, our ability to endure in our most challenging, weakest moments, even in times of victory, entirely and solely rests on God and His ability to do the impossible. The power that emanates from Him regenerates and powers us through any good or bad situation.

God can keep us. That is why the plan of salvation is not up to us but God. We may be able to endure for a while. Still, without God, in our lives, the self-generated endurance will turn into unhealthy pressure. That pressure becomes a destructive force that acts as a weapon of mass destruction to both the physical and spiritual man. We must, therefore, leave everything up to the one who is…

> *"able to keep us from falling, and to present us faultless before the presence of his glory with exceeding joy* **(Jude 1:24 KJV).***

It is His duty as God to protect us and to keep us.

> *"Know ye that the Lord he is God: it is he that hath made us, and not we ourselves; we are his people, and the sheep of his pasture. (Psalms 100:3 KJV). For it is God which worketh in you both to will and to do of his good pleasure* **(Philippians 2:13 KJV).**

He created us for His purpose, and He will never abandon us. He stood in our place and suffered abandonment that we will never have to experience what it feels like to be forsaken by God the Father. *For He hath said I would never leave you nor forsake you.* We can depend on the nature and character of God to stand true to His words in our times of need.

Call to Action

Stop depending on your strength to carry you through your times of adversity. When Paul was going through a pressing time, he said,

> *"For we would not, brethren, have you ignorant of our trouble which came to us in Asia, that we were pressed out of measure, above strength, insomuch that we despaired even of life: But we had the sentence of death in ourselves, that we should not trust in ourselves, but in God which raiseth the dead. (2 Corinthians 1:8-9 KJV)*

They did not rely on their strength; therefore, they were able to overcome because of God's power and strength. Trust in God to bring you through your season of difficulties.

DAY 18 - WHY WORRY?

John 14:1 KJV

Let not your heart be troubled: ye believe in God, believe also in me.

Why worry about the necessities of life? Worry consumes us and leads to questioning and doubt in God.

> *"This is why I tell you to never be worried about your life, for all that you need will be provided, such as food, water, clothing—everything your body needs. Isn't there more to your life than a meal? Isn't your body more than clothing?* **(Matthew 6:25 TPT).**

We are reminded daily through the wisdom and glory of God's creation that we can count on the character and immutable nature of God to provide what is necessary at the right moment.

> *"Look at all the birds—do you think they worry about their existence? They don't plant or reap or store up food, yet your heavenly Father provides them each with food. Aren't you much more valuable to your Father than they? "And why would you worry about your clothing? Look at all the beautiful flowers of the field. They don't work or toil, and yet not even Solomon in all his splendor was robed in beauty more than one of these!* **(Matthew 6:26-29 TPT).**

Take Abraham as a prime example of God's ability and power to provide for us at the right place, at the right time. God told Abraham to sacrifice his one and only son born to him and his wife through a promise God made with Abraham, for which he had to wait for 25 years. Some years after Isaac was born, God tested Abraham and told him to sacrifice his beloved son.

And it came to pass after these things, that God did tempt Abraham, and said unto him, Abraham: and he said, Behold, here I am. And he said, Take now thy son, thine only son Isaac, whom thou lovest, and get thee into the land of Moriah; and offer him there for a burnt offering upon one of the mountains which I will tell thee of. And Abraham rose up early in the morning, and saddled his ass, and took two of his young men with him, and Isaac his son, and clave the wood for the burnt offering, and rose up, and went unto the place of which God had told him. Then on the third day Abraham lifted up his eyes, and saw the place afar off. And Abraham said unto his young men, Abide ye here with the ass; and I and the lad will go yonder and worship, and come again to you. And Abraham took the wood of the burnt offering, and laid it upon Isaac his son; and he took the fire in his hand, and a knife; and they went both of them together. And Isaac spake unto Abraham his father, and said, My father: and he said, Here am I, my son. And he said, Behold the fire and the wood: but where is the lamb for a burnt offering? And Abraham said, My son, God will provide himself a lamb for a burnt offering: so they went both of them together. And they came to the place which God had told him of; and Abraham built an altar there, and laid the wood in order, and bound Isaac his son, and laid him on the altar upon the wood. And Abraham stretched forth his hand, and took the knife to slay his son.

And the angel of the Lord called unto him out of heaven, and said, Abraham, Abraham: and he said, Here am I. And he said, Lay not thine hand upon the lad, neither do thou any thing unto him: for now I know that thou fearest God, seeing thou hast not withheld thy son, thine only son from me. And Abraham lifted up his eyes, and looked, and behold behind him a ram caught in a thicket by his horns: and Abraham went and took the ram, and offered him up for a burnt offering in the stead of his son. And Abraham called the name of that place

Abraham trusted God to provide regardless of the complexity of his current situation. I can imagine Isaac looking around, wondering what his father will use as a sacrifice. When he asked Abraham about what he would use, knowing that his son would be the one to be offered, he responded otherwise by saying God will provide the lamb for the offering. Because of Abraham's faithfulness, we know God today as *Jehovah Jireh,* which means God, our provider. He provided for Abraham in a delicate time in his life, and he recorded the testament of God's provision that is with us even unto this day. God's demonstration of His power, love, care, and compassion is not just to man. His very creation should ignite our faith, filling us with the knowledge that we are so much more valuable to God. So, which one of you by worrying could add anything to your life? Trust in God; He will make a way.

Call to Action

We often sing the song, "Why worry when you can pray?" Trust Jesus, and He will lead the way. Don't be like doubting Thomas; put your faith and trust in Jesus. Why worry when you can pray? How many times have we taken this song for granted? I know I have. My charge to you is to trust in the Lord. It is human to worry, but when you start to worry, remind yourself of this song, use it as your mantra to spur your faith-filled response in worrying times.

DAY 19 - CAN YOU SWALLOW YOUR PRIDE AND FORGIVE?

Proverbs 29:23 KJV

A man's pride will bring him low,

But a humble spirit will obtain honor.

Life can be more comfortable for some of us if we only learn to swallow our pride and forgive. Most times, we experience torment in our lives, and our prayers go unanswered not because of the devil's schemes against us but because of our reluctance to acknowledge our shortcomings or where we have caused hurt and pain in the lives of others.

For if ye forgive men their trespasses, your heavenly Father will also forgive you: But if ye forgive not men their trespasses, neither will your Father forgive your trespasses **(Matthew 6:14-15KJV).**

Forgiveness is an essential character trait that every believer must demonstrate in his or her everyday life.

When we speak of forgiveness, we speak of Jesus, as He is the epitome of what forgiveness towards others means. He forgave us when He died for the redemption and liberty of humanity. The following scriptures demonstrate the love of God that abounds towards us.

"But God commendeth his love toward us, in that, while we were yet sinners, Christ died for us." **(Romans 5:8 KJV).**

Forgiveness is the key to living a healthy, peaceful spirit-filled life. Our inability to be held accountable for our shortcomings displays our flawed character, integrity, and failure to live a Christ-like life. Pride is a feeling of deep pleasure or satisfaction in achievement, an accomplishment, in someone, or something else. It is also conceit, egotism, vanity, vainglory, all over one's appearance or status in life and not just something that has been accomplished. It is an inwardly directed emotion that can easily offend others which carries a connotation that displays an inflated sense of one's worth or personal status. It typically makes one feel superior over others and can easily make someone look condescendingly at others.

When we fail to forgive, it shows how proud we are; our unwillingness to set aside how we feel in a particular moment to right whatever wrong we have done is a clear demonstration of our self-centeredness. Peace is one of the most valuable and rewarding feelings a person can ever have while on this Christian journey. Nothing is worth more to me than to have a life full of peace. Peace towards God, myself, family, friends, and just about anyone. Sadly, a lot of us lack the peace of God in our lives. We are tormented and frustrated each day because we fail to disassociate ourselves from our proud ways. The peace of God supersedes all understanding. No matter what situation we face, whatever happens to us, or whoever is responsible for the actions committed against us, we must take the necessary step to fix that situation. We should allow the Lord to work on our hearts to love our neighbors. That way, we will forgive them and be filled with God's peace. As the Word of God declares,

> *If it be possible, as much as lieth in you, live peaceably with all men.* **(Romans 12:18 KJV)**

> *Pride will get us nowhere. A man's pride shall bring him low: but honour shall uphold the humble in spirit.* **(Proverbs 29:23 KJV)**

I've had many things done to me by people, family, and close family friends that messed up my life big time, and one such thing was being sexually molested at the age of 12 by two brothers whose family was close friends of my family. That incident cost me my virginity. I did not get to decide for myself what I wanted to do with it. After that ordeal, my life practically changed not for the better but the worst, and that is where my journey into self-hate and sexual immorality began. I was scared and could not tell anyone or my family members what had happened to me even up to this day. Well,

I guess they will find out after reading this book. However, my point is that I did not understand at that age about forgiveness.

I spent most of my life in fear, condemnation, and low self-esteemed. I had days when I felt like committing suicide. It was not until I got older, quite frankly, when I got saved, that I understood what forgiveness is and how powerful and freeing forgiving and being forgiven can be. The crux of the matter is that Christ forgave me, I forgave myself, I also forgave those who carried out the act. I was free. I do not look at what happened to me anymore as a bad thing, and I am a better person today because of Jesus Christ. I am not afraid to talk about my experiences. Whatever I have gone through happened to me to help those who have experienced such things as I did.

Call to Action

Each time I go down to pray, I pray the words of this song by Kevin Levar, and I encourage you to do the same.

> I want a heart that forgives
> A heart full of love
> One with compassion just like Yours above
> One that overcomes evil with goodness and love
> Like it never happened, never holding a grudge
> I want a heart that forgives that lives and let's lives
> One that keeps loving over and over again
> One that men can't offend
> Because Your word is within
> One that loves without price like You Lord Jesus Christ
> I want a heart that loves everybody, even my enemies
> I wanna love like You, be like You, just like You did

I wanna heart that forgives

Wanna heart that forgives
When the ones that are closest
That I've known the longest hurt me the most
I still wanna love them just like You loved me
Even though I'm hurting

I wanna heart that forgives
When the pain is so deep
And it's so hard to speak about it to anyone
Just like Your Son, I give up my right
To hold it against them with hatred inside
I wanna heart that loves everybody, even my enemies
I wanna love like You, be like You, just like You did
I wanna walk like You, talk like You, just like You did
Wanna be like You, live like You, just like You did
Cause the heart that forgives is the heart that will live
Totally free from the pain of the past
And the heart that lets go
Is the heart that will know so much freedom

Excerpt from **A HEART THAT FORGIVES** (Levar Burton & One Sound; Album – Let's
Come Together (Deluxe Edition); Released 2010)

DAY 20 - PRAYING WITH THE RIGHT WORDS

> **Luke 11:1 KJV**
>
> And it came to pass, that, as he was praying in a certain place, when he ceased, one of his disciples said unto him, Lord, teach us to pray, as John also taught his disciples.

Do you have times when it is hard for you to find the right words to pray? No matter how much you try, the right words sometimes never seem to come. However, is there such a thing as praying with the right words? It seems that it would be coming from ourselves, as we would be giving every thought to the things we say. We are timely reminded that;

"When you pray, there is no need to repeat empty phrases, praying like those who don't know God, for they expect God to hear them because of their many words. **(Matthew 6:7 TPT)**

"And when you pray, do not heap up empty phrases as the Gentiles do, for they think that they will be heard for their many words **(Matthew 6:7 ESV).**

Prayer is not meditation or passive reflection; it is a direct address to God. It is the communication of the human soul with the Lord who created the soul. When we enter the presence of the Lord, we should do so with openness and complete vulnerability in humility before Him. This gives us the perfect opportunity for direct, honest, and unfiltered communication with God through prayer. When we open ourselves to God through pure dialogue, we can meaningfully say *'nevertheless not my will'* in sincerity and truth.

Over the years, from my own experiences, I have found out that the more vulnerable I get while in prayer, the more aware I become of my desperate need for God in my life. I see that I can be or do nothing without Him, and without His guidance and strength, I would be lost and weak. Being open in the presence of God has allowed me to feel free to talk to Him, and I am confident that He is listening. Not only that, but it enables me to be honest with myself and others about my feelings, weaknesses, and what is going on in my life.

There are even times when I feel Him moving all over me and in me, working on me. It is easy to become flustered with the different trends of prayers that we see nowadays, which, nothing is wrong with it because there is a time and place for everything. You may feel as though you are not touching heaven if your face is not disfigured, and you are not gasping for breath at each word, shooting fire from your eyes, or blooding up the devil's kingdom. But my friend, that's far from the truth. I used to feel that way, but I am comforted by the words of Peter the Apostle when he said;

> *"For the eyes of the Lord are over the righteous, and his ears are open unto their prayers: but the face of the Lord is against them that do evil. (1 Peter 3:12 KJV).*

I can pray with the assurance that God is listening. So when the time comes, and we fail with words to pray, fret not thyself for in the self-same hour the Spirit helps us in our weakness.

*"For we do not know what to pray for as we ought, but the Spirit himself intercedes for us with groanings too deep for words **(Romans 8:26 ESV)**.*

Think not of prayer in a complicated way because it is not. It is just how you would freely speak to your best friend or someone you genuinely love.

Call to Action

Be yourself the next time you go to pray. God is not looking for fancy tailor-made words; He is looking for you to pour out your heart to Him. Everything that you feel, experience, think, or did, God wants to have that unfiltered talk with you today. So put down your borrowed words and empty phrases and talk to a real God in a real way.

DAY 21 - IT MAKES NO SENSE, BUT STILL REJOICE

1 Thessalonians 5:16 KJV

Rejoice always;

Life will consistently have its fair share of problems. In any case, there are a few circumstances that we experience that make it hard for us to rejoice. What is there to rejoice about after being diagnosed with stage 4 cancer? How can you rejoice when the bills are due, your home will be repossessed, and the bank has denied you to pay your home loan? There is no food in the house, broken relationships, issues in your marriage, death, and numerous things that accompany life? For the unbelievers, it is misery and pain. But the individuals who have faith in a Sovereign God will encounter peace, hope, glory, and happiness.

There is so much to rejoice about despite our misfortunes and circumstances,

> *"for I consider that the sufferings of this present time are not worth comparing with the glory that is to be revealed to us* **(Romans 8:18 NIV)**.

With this truth, we can rejoice in our sufferings.

> *...knowing that suffering produces endurance, and endurance produces character, and character produces hope, and hope does not put us to shame, because God's love has been poured into our hearts*

Since we have the love of God in our hearts, we should seek to trust God wholeheartedly.

There is an old saying, "that misery loves company," so think about the other unfortunate situations that we call down on ourselves if we neglect to trust in God. We rejoice through troublesome periods since it shows absolute dependence on the God of heaven that can do the exceeding, abundantly impossible. Jesus is all-powerful. He is mighty to save. We should give God thanks for all that He is doing in our lives. On most occasions, due to our uncertainty, which blinds us, we fail to see what God is doing for us through our sufferings. In scripture, the reality we have come to see is that He always has a plan and His thoughts towards us are pure and perfect.

Truly! His ways are past finding out. You can rely on Him to come through for you. Indeed, His thoughts are higher than your musings, yet you can believe that His will is consistently ideal for those He has called and loved. I realize it is difficult for us to practice confidence amid our circumstances since everything we can see is the situation's cutoff time. You are left to contemplate whether He will come through on schedule or leave us to confront the present circumstance alone. Yet,

"he hath said I will never leave you nor forsake you
(Hebrews 13:5 KJV).

Have faith in God, believe in His promises, and have faith in His words. You cannot give up on Him, and you cannot back down now! Even if you are in the valley, He will find a way through your difficulties to rescue you, so trust Him today. David said,

"If I take the wings of the morning and dwell in the
utter most part of the sea; even if I make my bed in
hell behold thou art there. Even there shall thy hand
lead me, and thy right hand shall hold me (Psalm
139:8-9 KJV).

When we pour out our hearts to God, we have confidence that He hears us, we feel so much more assured because we know that no matter what the problem or situation maybe He loves us and will do anything according to His perfect will just for us. I pray that our prayer and heart's desire is to be filled with an abundance of praise to sing unto the Lord whether in good or bad times, whether we are happy or sad for all the rest of our days. I am confident that God will secure us. I trust in His love and capable abilities to establish and uphold, and fill us with the strength and enduring capacity to withstand any storm, walk through any fire, and conquer any giant.

I believe that one day when He comes, we will gain our crown; we will fall at his feet, casting all our life before Him in perfect worship to the king. Be encouraged, my brothers and sisters.

Call to Action

"Rejoice in the Lord alway: and again I say, Rejoice. Be careful for nothing; but in everything by prayer and supplication with thanksgiving let your requests be made known unto God. And the peace of God, which passeth all understanding, shall keep your hearts and minds through Christ Jesus **(Philippians 4:4-7 KJV).**

DAY 22 - WHEN I LOSE SIGHT OF MY COMMISSIONED MISSION

Mark 16:15-17 NKJV

He said to them, "Go into all the world and preach the gospel to all creation. Whoever believes and is baptized will be saved, but whoever does not believe will be condemned. And these signs will accompany those who believe: In my name they will drive out demons; they will speak in new tongues;

Though not often, I tend to lose sight of why I was born again. Yes, we are all created to give God glory, and according to ***Ecclesiastes 12:13 "The whole duty of man is to fear God and keep his commandments (ESV).*** However, we are humans, and ever so often, we easily forget. The Lord has done a marvelous thing for us beyond our capacity to repay when He saved us. In case we fail to remember, we are commissioned to *'Go.'* We are branded as ambassadors and given the ministry of reconciliation. We have a restored relationship with God through Jesus Christ. We need to broadcast the gospel to those who do not know Christ, and we must declare that sin will keep us from having a relationship with God. However, the forgiveness of sins is available in Christ.

Jesus' perfect sacrifice on the cross made atonement for sin and brought harmony to mankind's relationship with Him. Jesus reconciled us to God. Now we can proclaim that people can repent of their sin and be right with God again through faith in Jesus. We are called to win souls for Christ and absolutely no one is exempt.

*"He came not to call the righteous but sinners unto repentance **(Luke 5:32 KJV).***

*For God so loved the world that he gave his only-begotten son that whosoever believeth In him should not perish but have everlasting life **(John 3:16 KJV).***

We have to evoke the change necessary for our light to shine that men may see the works we do and glorify the Father, which is in heaven.

This blessed assurance that we have in Jesus Christ; unearths a type of anointing that transcends the very definition of our human feelings and existence. It unleashes a kind of joy that the world and its pleasures cannot give nor comprehend and is only attainable and available exclusively to the children of God. If you so desire to be a part of this effervescent spiritual awakening, you MUST! Therefore, be BORN AGAIN! The experience of being born again is a supernatural life-changing event that will resuscitate you from your deadness brought about by sin. As it is written,

*"And you hath he quickened, who were dead in trespasses and sins; **(Ephesians 2:1 KJV).***

The process of being born again is simple. Repent of your sins, which is to acknowledge, confess, and abandon your evil ways and turn to God and be baptized. After which, you will receive the life-giving spirit of Jesus through the Holy Spirit's infilling that is all done in His name - Jesus Christ. **(Acts 2:38 KJV).** A friendly reminder to those who have already accepted Jesus as their personal savior, never forget that,

> *"you have been born again [that is, reborn from above—spiritually transformed, renewed, and set apart for His purpose] not of seed which is perishable but [from that which is] imperishable and immortal, that is, through the living and everlasting Word of God. For, "All flesh is like grass, And all its glory like the flower of grass. The grass withers And the flower falls off, But the word of the Lord endures forever." And this is the word [the good news of salvation] which was preached to you.* **(1 Peter 1:23-25 AMP)***

Call to Action

Now is the time to shift your focus on what is most important, and that is taking up the responsibility given to us the moment we were saved. What is it that you can do to spread the gospel to those you interact with daily? How can you share the message of Jesus Christ to someone today? Find creative ways to tell someone about the saving power available to anyone who desires to accept Jesus as their personal Lord and savior.

DAY 23 - WHERE DO I FIT?

Proverbs 18:24 AMP

The man of too many friends [chosen indiscriminately] will be broken in pieces and come to ruin, But there is a [true, loving] friend who [is reliable and] sticks closer than a brother.

When we are out with friends, we get so caught up in the moment that we tend to lose ourselves. Oh, that has never happened to you. Well, it has certainly happened to me more than once. I had to take a step back to assess my life and look at how I represented Christ. This introspection led me to make decisions I was not comfortable with, but having weighed in the balance what values more, my friends or Christ though not easy, I chose Christ because my behavior was entirely against His will. When you are with your friends, do they see Jesus in you? Are your actions and conversations as becometh saints, or do they betray you? Is your light shining in the midst of them? Or are you drawn away by their negative influence or your lust?

One important thing to note is, wherever we find ourselves in life, whether in our home, school, church or even on the job, we must be the ones to effect change in our surroundings and not our surroundings changing us.

"if sinners entice you, turn your back on them! **(Proverbs 1:10 NLT)**

*Let your speech always be gracious, seasoned with salt, so that you may know how you ought to answer each person **(Colossians 4:6 ESV)**.*

Not every company will be the right company; neither will every friendship yield positive growth results.

It is not my intention to discourage anyone from having friends, whether in the church or outside of the church, but we must be cautious with our choices, as it will have its impact on our lives negatively and or positively.

*"Do not make friends with a hot-tempered man, do not associate with one easily angered, or you may learn his ways and get yourself ensnared **(Proverbs 22:24 NIV)**.*

*A man of many companions may come to ruin, but there is a friend who sticks closer than a brother **(Proverbs 18:24 ESV)**.*

Ask the Lord to help you choose the friends He sees fit for your life. In all your ways, acknowledge Him, and He will direct your path no matter how small it may be. It is easy for us to forget that the things we consider simple or small in our lives are known and matters to God. I used to believe that I do not have to go to God about everything, that is, of course, until I learned the hard way through many disappointments, hurt, and setbacks that could have been easily avoided had I talked to God about the decisions I made. It is essential for us to consider the character of the people we allow in our lives.

Not everyone that comes into our lives will be uplifting or supportive, and yes, we call them friends.

Choose people who share the same interest as you do when it comes to your walk with God. Choose friends who will push you and positively motivate you towards your dreams, friends who will watch out for you in danger and stand with you in times of struggles. Friends who will pray with you when you have let down your guard in moments of weakness and friends who are not afraid to call you out when you go against the will of God or violate your conscience. You may be wondering, do people like this exist in these times? Unbelievably, yes, they do exist, but by ourselves, we cannot find them so easily. That is why we need God's guidance to direct us to these people or to direct them to us.

I would also like to mention that we can be very shallow in our thoughts about where these persons may come from. God can weed out the best of friends from the most unlikely places that we would have never thought to be of great blessings to our lives. Do not discredit the wisdom, knowledge, and power of God to provide for us in any way that we lack. God says, Ask, and it shall be given. Therefore, if you find yourself around a group of people, you call friends, and you have to make excuses about your faith, or if you do something good to glorify God in their midst and afterwards you feel ashamed, then get you better people, they are not your friends.

Call to Action

Ask God to show you that one person or the persons that will best compliment His intended will for your life to bring it to fruition.

DAY 24 - REGRETS, REGRETS, REGRETS

Philippians 3:13 NASB

Brothers and sisters, I do not regard myself as having taken hold of it yet; but one thing I do: forgetting what lies behind and reaching forward to what lies ahead,

Do you have regrets? Because I do. From time to time, I do something, or things may happen to me that I later regret. We all have regrets, the shame of our past, sins committed, being born, meeting certain people, being in some relationships, working at some establishments, performing specific tasks, or even saying certain things. Regrets about waking up, the poor decisions we make which results in the life we now live et cetera. I do not believe that anyone, dead or alive, has never had regrets at some point in time. Regret is sorrow or remorse over something that has happened or that we have done. Regret can also be a sense of disappointment over what has not happened, such as regretting wasted years. To be human is to have regrets because making mistakes is a universal experience. Great men of old experienced moments of regret in their lives. Peter, for example is one of the persons who was extremely sorry and regretful of a foolish decision he made.

Despite the many times that Jesus told His disciples that he would be betrayed and then later crucified, they never truly understood nor believed that Jesus would have suffered such a fate by the hands of His own people. Peter was one of Jesus' disciples who was deeply devoted to Jesus, so much so that even when Jesus told Peter that he would deny Him ***Peter said unto him, Though I should die with thee, yet will I not deny thee. Likewise also said all the*** *disciples. (Matthew 26:35) KJV*. When the time had come for Jesus to be betrayed into the hands of sinners, at the point of his arrest, Peter showed his devotion to the Jesus by cutting off the ear of one of the soldiers *(John 18:10) KJV*. This more than proved his loyalty, but it was not enough to allow the words of Jesus spoken before concerning Peter's betrayal to return unto Him void. When Peter came to the realization that all that Jesus spoke to them afore time concerning His impending fate has now become a reality, fear made Peter run away when the soldiers arrested Jesus, and later denied his Lord. He deeply regretted his actions and wept bitterly.

Esau is another biblical figure who miserably regretted his decision to sell his birthright to his brother Jacob. The bible recorded that he found no place of repentance even thou he sought it with much tears. *(Hebrews 12:15-17) KJV.*

Most, if not everyone is familiar with the story of Job. The events that took place in his life though sanctioned by God were rather unfortunate. Even though Job gave God thanks for all that had befallen him, there came a moment in his life where he regretted the day that he was born. There is a saying in Jamaica that says, *"Pressure buss pipe"*. It is always said when you are faced with a situation that has caused you to somehow reach your limit or breaking point and at this point in Job's life, his outburst of regret for the day in which he was born signified that he had a *'pressure buss pipe moment'*. **Job, after this, opened his mouth and cursed the day of his birth. "Let** *the day on which I was born perish, And the night which announced: 'There is a man-child conceived.' May that day be darkness; Let God above not care about it, Nor light shine on it. "Why did I not die at birth, Come forth from the womb and expire? Why did the knees receive me? And why the breasts, that I would nurse? For now I would have lain down and been quiet; I would have slept then, I would have been at rest [in death] (Job 3:1-4 KJV).*

Judas Iscariot was one of Jesus' disciples, which means that he was exposed to all the teachings, miracles, and great works of Jesus. There was no denying that he was not present when Peter got the revelation that Jesus Christ is indeed the son of God. Yet still, he had a different agenda and that was revealed when he chose to betray Jesus. After he realized what he had done, Judas was so filled with regret that he tried to return the money he took from the Chief Priests and Elders. When they refused to accept the 30 pieces of silver, he cast away the money, went out, and killed himself.

Even God being perfect yet at some point had regrets. In a couple of places, we are told that God "regretted" an action He took. The Hebrew root for the word "regret" actually means "To sigh." Since we know God does not make mistakes, the concept of sighing is a more descriptive term *for the kind of regret God experiences. In **Genesis 6:7, it says that, after seeing the wickedness on the earth, God regretted making man (KJV).** Therefore, this does not mean that the Lord felt that He made a mistake in creating human beings, but His heart was sorrowful as He witnessed the direction they were going. Since God knows everything beforehand, He already knew that sin would bring consequences, so He was not surprised by it. Instead, this glimpse into God's character shows us that, even though He already knows we will sin, it still grieves Him when we choose to sin against him.*

Human regret is different from Godly sorrow. Human regret occurs because we do not know all things, and we do make mistakes. As we age, we often look back on decisions made in our youth and regret our choices. However, those regrets usually fall into one of two categories. Our regrets arise from either foolish choices or sinful choices, and each requires a different response.

---

https://www.gotquestions.org/dealing-with-regrets.html

Call to Action

While it is human to feel regret, we must do our best to live life with purpose and meaning. I charge you this day to make careful decisions to limit the regrets you may face in your life.

DAY 25 - WHAT IF? AND WHAT IS?

Psalm 124:1 NLT

What if the LORD had not been on our side? Let all Israel repeat:...

Stop focusing on the "What-ifs" and focus more on your "What-is". Some time ago, I got some bad news about a friend who met in an accident and his truck overturned. It shook me to my core. Instantly, my whole life flashed before my eyes with the thought of the absence of him not being a part of my life anymore. Even though the accident's outcome was not severe or fatal in any way, it still got me thinking,

WHAT IF?

- What if the accident was fatal?
- What if we had an argument before the accident and I didn't forgive him?
- What if he had damaged someone's property or broke something expensive?
- What if the vehicle had exploded after being over-turned?
- What if I didn't get to see him at the hospital?

What if? What if? What if?

My mind was racing with what-ifs so much that I could not even process the miracle of his escape without severe injuries. Did you say miraculous? Yes, a blessing, that's what it was, because God had stepped in. I started to silently and slowly thank God while I regrouped my thoughts and quieted myself, resurfacing from drowning in them. As I did, I heard it loud and clear in my spirit, *Stop focusing on the "What-ifs" of your situations and focus more on your "What-is"*. The good thing about the bad news was that it was not so bad after all because he and his traveling companions were safe, narrowly escaping death. Illuminated by these truths and how God had graciously saved His people my *what-ifs* began to fade revealing *what-is*. The *what-is* - was that they were safe, no harm had come to them. God protected them, and they had an opportunity at life and wellness again marked by the testimony of God's goodness.

So many times, we find ourselves in mind-blowing situations, near-death experiences, unexpected setbacks, being at the wrong place at the wrong time, numerous life challenges. However, even though we may narrowly escape them or get past them, within the moment, it is hard to think about the positives of what is happening. Nonetheless, as soon as we are free from the gnawing thoughts of the situation, and we give ourselves over into thinking, that is when the *what-ifs* start to take you over. Instead of focusing on the *what-ifs*, take a moment to quiet yourself, look at what is around you, then look at yourself and start to give God thanks for *what-is*.

WHAT IS

- *What is* - you are safe from the storm.
- *What is* - you are ok despite your setbacks.

- *What is* - God provided at the last second even though you are out of a job.

- *What is-* God loves you even though you feel all alone.

- *What is* - focusing on the good in every bad situation will reveal God's mighty hand and His sovereignty at work amid the storm. Maybe you were set up to die, but you are not. You are alive, so focus on the what-is of the situation instead of the what- if. You lost your job, but you still got some money in the bank to last you for a while. Give God thanks. God will provide. He will take care of you. Just trust Him because it is already done.

Call to Action

Pray and do not worry, thank Him for the victory you have the authority in Jesus. What is important is what God is doing and where He has taken you from. No longer do you have to wonder what could have happened if God never stepped in at the time He did.

DAY 26 - FOR YOU SEE YOUR CALLING BRETHREN

> 1 Corinthians 1:27-31TPT
>
> But God chose those whom the world considers foolish to shame those who think they are wise, and God chose the puny and powerless to shame the high and mighty. He chose the lowly, the laughable in the world's eyes—nobodies—so that he would shame the somebodies. For he chose what is regarded as insignificant in order to supersede what is regarded as prominent, so that there would be no place for prideful boasting in God's presence. For it is not from man that we draw our life but from God as we are being joined to Jesus, the Anointed One. And now he is our God-given wisdom, our virtue, our holiness, and our redemption. And this fulfills what is written: If anyone boasts, let him only boast in all that the Lord has done!

If every time the world sinks its claws of the perpetual challenges you may face in your life, and your only defense against this is to run away or give up, you will never achieve growth. You will never have the opportunity to perfect your stance to fight.

Be alert, stand firm in the faith,

be brave, be strong (1 Corinthians 16:13 GNT).

Running away or giving up does not yield growth. It turns you into a coward, and you will never know what it feels like to be victorious. God calls cowards, but He does not keep them. Through His unfeigned character and His immutable righteousness, He justifies the cowardly and changes him from the inside out to be bold through Him. All twelve disciples of Jesus were just ordinary men who had regular day jobs like us today. Without Christ in their lives, nothing else was super special about them that influenced God's decision to choose them as His disciples.

However, if you read the gospel according to John, you would realize that Jesus had many followers. After He (Jesus) declared Himself to be the bread of life *(the bread being His flesh which they should eat thereof and His blood also which they should drink thereof)*, this saying troubled some of them, and many of His followers turned from following Him that day. He then asked the twelve whether they would also turn from following Him, but they chose to stay with Jesus because they believe that He has the words to eternal life. *(John 6:48-71 KJV)*

There is nothing super special about us outside of Christ that propels or influences God to choose those that are saved. God extends an open invitation to all to come unto Him. It is, therefore, our responsibility whether we want to accept His call. Each of the twelve disciples made their own decision to follow Jesus when He called them. Some of them were literally on the job when He extended the invitation to follow Him. They abandoned their livelihood and began to follow someone I suppose they were not even at the moment sure was the Messiah that was to come. However, I believe that there is something different about the calling of Jesus; when convicted, it is almost impossible to resist.

There is no room for discrimination in the kingdom of God. In the sight of God, all flesh is equal and loved the same. God called fishermen, doctors, tax collectors, and the world's most learned men. All these men were used for His glory.

While Jesus was having dinner at Matthew's house, many tax collectors and sinners came and ate with him and his disciples. [11] When the Pharisees saw this, they asked his disciples, "Why does your teacher eat with tax collectors and sinners?"

No one is exempt from the call of God. When Jesus was on earth, His association was not with the wealthy and well-learned men because they reeked of self-righteousness. Rather, He was found mostly among the sinners and those considered outcasts, the scum of the earth. The Pharisees often questioned Jesus' involvement with them, and they even went further to insult Jesus by saying He was gluttonous, and a winebibber *(Matt. 11:19 KJV).* Nevertheless, Jesus had an agenda. He came to do the will of His father.

*"For I have come down from heaven, not to do My own will, but the will of Him who sent Me" **(John 6:38 KJV).***

His will constitutes us. He came not to call those who think of themselves as being enough or those who believe that they do not need God. He did not call the rich or upper class of society who believes that they have life and all things figured out.

...instead, God chose things the world considers foolish in order to shame those who think they are wise. And he chose things that are powerless to

Call to Action

The next time you are faced with the challenges of life and you are tempted to run away or give up, and like Gideon, you think to yourself that you are weak and small, remind yourself of who you are and whose you are, then take your stand and fight! Keep in mind that in all life's difficulties, you are more than conquerors through Him that loved us.

> *If God be for us who can be against us?* **(Romans 8:31 KJV)**

DAY 27 - WOULD GOD INTENTIONALLY HURT ME?

> **Hebrews 12:6-7 NIV**
>
> because the Lord disciplines the one he loves, and he chastens everyone he accepts as his son." Endure hardship as discipline; God is treating you as his children. For what children are not disciplined by their father?

Due to the many unfortunate events that have happened in my life it has led me to ask myself this question, would God intentionally hurt me? The word intentional denotes something that is done on purpose, or deliberately. So then, I had to ask myself this question because I was so pressed beyond measure. I had to fight many battles one after the other. I cannot say that I have experienced any rest from fighting because the devil was and still is adamant in seeing the destruction of my life and the loss of my soul. There were many days when I questioned whether God loved me or not, and if He loved me why would He allow so much evil to befall me? I have come to realize that whatsoever befalls me, the sovereign God exercises total control and authority over my life; and as His child, it is His responsibility to take care of me. His care exclusively involves His guidance, protection, provision, love, grace, mercy, all of which are wrapped up in the promises of God found in His Word.

God would never intentionally bring harm to those He loves, nor will He allow the enemy to work through others to hurt us to the point of being unable to recover or to the point of death. Yes! The bible tells us that *whom the Lord loveth He chasteneth*. To chasten is to discipline, punish, especially to improve someone's behavior. It can also mean to tame, subdue, moderate, or restrain someone's actions. In all cases, it typically involves some form of discipline or negative consequences for the person being chastened. God sends trials to people whom He truly loves, it is a universal norm. Of course, this does not imply that He sends unjustified chastisement or that He sends it "for the only goal" of inflicting suffering. That cannot be. But it also implies that His chastisements demonstrate His parental concern for us. He does not treat us as a father typically treats an illegitimate child: with neglect and indifference. The fact that He corrects us reveals that He has fatherly feelings for us and exerts paternal care toward us.

This is the truth I have come to know and learn as I go through my daily trials. When we read the account of Job's life and what he had to go through, anyone who does not understand the God that we serve would quickly dismiss Him as a God who is unkind. I had that mindset once because I did not know God for myself; neither did I understand His ways. The trials that we face and the unfortunate situation and incidents that the Lord allows to happen in our lives are only to make us strong. ***These trials are only to test your faith, to see whether or not it is strong and pure. It is being tested as fire tests gold and purifies it—and your faith is far more precious to God than mere gold; so if your faith remains strong after being tried in the test tube of fiery trials, it will bring you much praise and glory and honor on the day of his return. (1 Peter 1:7 KJV).*** God purposely corrects us when we make mistakes, and places us in situations that we can use for spiritual development.

Understanding that God's will for our lives is to bring about growth and an expected end for us, we should know that the enemy's plans to destroy our lives are all monitored and known to God. Whatever is allowed in our lives, we must realize that God is sovereign and exercises control over everything. Let us, therefore, examine a famous scripture quoted by everyone, Christians, and non-Christians alike. *Isaiah 54:17* declares that;

No weapon that is formed against you shall prosper. Every tongue which rises against you in judgment You shall condemn (KJV).

Weapons will form, but as long as God does not consent for those weapons to harm you, it WILL NOT prosper. People will talk, that is what they do, but their negative speech against your life HAS ALREADY been condemned by the power of the spoken Word of God. So take courage in knowing that the good Lord fights for you. He will never intentionally hurt you. Just as an earthly father would discipline their child or children, so our heavenly Father deals with us as sons. ***Now no chastening for the present seemeth to be joyous, but grievous: nevertheless afterward it yieldeth the peaceable fruit of righteousness unto them which are exercised thereby. (Hebrews 12:11KJV)***

Call to Action

It is human to question the things that may happen to us in life. While this is the case, the devil plans to trick us into thinking that God does not love us. That is why we are faced with these challenges. But that is a lie from the pit of hell! Whenever you start to wonder if God is punishing you or is out to get you because of something you may have done or due to circumstances that may befall you, speak with authority, and rebuke the devil. The Lord would never intentionally hurt us. He loves us with an everlasting love. The devil seeks only to corrupt your thoughts about our sovereign God.

DAY 28 - BE NOT AFRAID OF THEIR FACES

The world that we live in is a sick, sad world where the power of darkness roams, a world where injustice resides, and pride presides over men's hearts and affairs. Men are not fazed by their kind anymore, so you find that they will do the most heinous and hurtful things to each other, and this drives fear into people. I look at them, and some of their distorted faces *(what they consider to be tough)* would scare you away if you never knew they were just mere mortal men. Nevertheless, I know one who is not fazed by our frailty. One who cannot be compared to man for He is God. God is the only supreme being of high authority and incalculable sovereign supremacy who made us all in His glorious image and likeness, intentionally creating us the way His spirit delights. He is not afraid of us; instead, the Lord loves us and pities us because we seldom understand who we are and what the power of sin can do to us.

We put on the tough-guy act to scare those who do not know the God above. Sometimes this act of being tough is our best shield or guard against our flaws that we use to cover up or hide behind. It is a pity that those who are afraid of bullies do not know that bullies are scared of themselves and their imperfections. Hence, they provoke and endanger others' lives to feel a sense of gratification and pleasure, which they hope to use as a guise to excuse their shortcomings.

No matter who you are, whether a murderer, thief, liar, gang member, bully, drug lord, etc., you are only scaring yourself and putting your own lives in danger. One day, it will not matter how tough you may be or the awful things you may have done; we all will recognize who is superior and in control over all things, and his name is Jesus. All will see that He is Lord. We will eventually reach to a point in time

> *"That at the name of Jesus every knee should bow, of things in heaven, and things in earth, and things under the earth; And that every tongue should confess that Jesus Christ is Lord, to the glory of God the Father.* **(Philippians 2:10-11 KJV)**

Call to Action

Fear is of the devil, so therefore this leaves no room for you to be afraid of the faces of men. For some of us, when we go out to witness, we shy away because we are so scared of men's faces and reactions. Even so, I urge you today be not afraid of their faces. Instead, be kind and show them love no matter what. Ask the Lord to give you boldness to face each person you will encounter.

DAY 29 - CHECK OUT MY STORY

Hebrews 12:1 KJV

Looking unto Jesus the author and finisher of our faith; who for the joy that was set before him endured the cross, despising the shame, and is set down at the right hand of the throne of God.

We are the ones who will choose what story our lives will tell whether it is a story of victory or one of defeat. While Jesus is the author and the finisher of our faith, the outcome of the ***settings, characters, plot, conflict, and theme*** of our life's story will depend entirely on us. Meaning, how we choose to respond to the many challenges and situations that life offers will tell how our story ends.

THE SETTING

Where and when is the story set? Setting represents both the physical location but also the time (i.e., past, present, future) and the social and cultural conditions in which the characters exist.[1]

The setting of our life is where God has placed us. Over time, we see that based on God's will and man's various decisions, the setting of our lives' can be easily changed by moving to a new location for a home, job, death, etc. We must remain in God's will for His desired purpose and plan for our lives to be accomplished. If we want our story to be one of victory, then the safest place to be is in the will of God and where He has strategically placed us for His will to be manifest. We often experience defeat when choosing to follow the

---

[1] https://www.dreamerswriting.com/elements-of-a-story/

path we feel is the right way to take. However, we are constantly reminded by God's Word that,

> *"...our lives are not our own. We are not able to plan our own course **(Jeremiah 10:23 NLT).***

> *There is a way that seems right to a man, but its end is the way to death **(Proverbs 14:12 ESV).***

CHARACTER

A person, animal, or really anything personified. There can be one main character or many, and often there are secondary characters, but not always.[2]

The characters that are involved in our story are those persons who are a part of our lives. In our lives, we have set persons who will always be there like our families. Moreover, based on the type of path that you will choose for your life, along the way, you will see different persons entering into your life at other times and seasons to carry out their particular purpose in those moments. If you watch a movie or read a book, you will realize that not all the characters listed will be there until the end of the film or story. As Christians, people come into our lives for many different reasons. Some will be there until the end, and some will only be around for a short time. Whether long or

---

[2] https://www.dreamerswriting.com/elements-of-a-story/

short, seasonal or not, we need to be careful who we allow to be a part of our life's story from the beginning to the end. The people we choose will have a significant impact on our lives and the decisions that we make. If we make the wrong decisions, then we will be shaping a story of defeat, and if we make the right choices, then we are on our way to victory. We must allow God to help us to choose the right persons that will help us to shape our stories.

> *"A man of many companions may come to ruin, but there is a friend who sticks closer than a brother* **(Proverbs 18:24 ESV).**

> *Make no friendship with a man given to anger, nor go with a wrathful man, lest you learn his ways and entangle yourself in a snare* **(Proverbs 22:24 ESV).**

PLOT

The plot consists of the events that happen in the story. In a plot, you typically find an introduction, rising action, a climax, the falling action, and a resolution.[3]

Our life's story plot involves the many challenges, events, and roller coaster rides that life will throw at us. Earlier, we looked at the settings and characters in our lives, and there we see that each is interconnected for us to have an adequately composed story.

---

[3] https://www.dreamerswriting.com/elements-of-a-story/

conversely, the plot makes it more interesting, so much more like our lives because of the many twists, surprises, and unexpected events that can and will happen. It is necessary that we go through trials as Christians.

*Everyone who wants to live a godly life in Christ Jesus will be persecuted **(2 Timothy 3:12 ESV)**.*

Nonetheless, the most important thing about this is how we respond to the challenges that will arise.

CONFLICT

Every story must have a conflict, i.e., a challenge or problem around which the plot is based. Without conflict, the story will have no purpose or trajectory.[4]

It is said that for a story to be interesting, there needs to be conflict. Who would want to read a book or watch a movie that has no form of struggle against another character, against the forces of nature, against society, or even against something inside himself or herself (feelings, emotions, illness)? Still, this does make everything more appealing to read or watch. As Christians, we have our battles, and every day we must deal with ourselves, the constant war that goes on with the spirit and our flesh. There are forces of darkness, unfairness, and injustice of our society, even conflicts with our friends and loved ones. As hard as disputes can be, sometimes it makes our

---

[4] https://www.dreamerswriting.com/elements-of-a-story/

life interesting. We learn from these unfortunate events, and the lessons that we learn are often so valuable that we could have never leaned it anywhere else than through the difficulties we face. While we encounter conflicts as Christians, our response and actions towards such misfortunes should be as the Word of God declares,

"Do all that you can to live in peace with everyone (Romans 12:18 NLT).

Bear with one another and, if one has a complaint against another, forgiving each other; as the Lord has forgiven you, so you also must forgive **(Colossians 3:13 ESV).**

THEME

The Idea, belief, moral, lesson or insight – It is the central argument that the author is trying to make the reader understand. The theme is the "why" of the story.[5]

In every story or movie, there is always a lesson for us to learn. It is always close to the end or at the end of a story that the persons involved would understand why they were at a particular place *(settings),* why they had to encounter or end up with the persons they have in their lives *(character).* Alternatively, the many surprises, unfortunate incidents, breakups, fights, twists, and turns they had to

---

[5] https://www.dreamerswriting.com/elements-of-a-story/

go through *(plot)*. The many battles they had to face to make it to where they are now *(conflicts),* which leads us to the story's theme, the lesson learned having gone through such difficult trials. As Christians, we will never fully understand why we go through certain situations.

We will never fully understand why we had to suffer in a particular way, why we had to make certain sacrifices and give up certain friends or jobs. Why we had to move or lose some family by death and the list goes on. We will never fully understand why God has allowed all these things in our lives or why we are still going through them, but at the end of it all,

> *"...when he hath tried us, we shall come forth as gold **(Job 23:10 KJV).***

The bible declares that.

> *"For now [in this time of imperfection] we see in a mirror dimly [a blurred reflection, a riddle, an enigma], but then [when the time of perfection comes we will see reality] face to face. Now I know in part [just in fragments], but then I will know fully, just as I have been fully known [by God] **(1 Corinthians 13:12 AMP).***

As the definition states, the theme is the "Why" of the story. God is meticulously writing our stories as we speak. Each day a new page or chapter is being written of our lives. We need to understand that God knows us more than we know ourselves. He knows everything about our lives and what He does, where He puts us, what He gives us to do, and what He allows us to encounter is for our good.

> *All things work together for good to them that love God, to them who are the called according to his purpose **(Romans 8:28 KJV)**.*

> *According as he hath chosen us in him before the foundation of the world, that we should be holy and without blame before him in love: Having predestinated us unto the adoption of children by Jesus Christ to himself, according to the good pleasure of his will, To the praise of the glory of his grace, wherein he hath made us accepted in the beloved **(Ephesians 1:4-6 KJV)**.*

God loves us, and He will never put us in a position to hurt us to the point of no return. So today, remember that God is the author and finisher of our faith. An author is the creator or originator of any written work. More broadly defined, an author is "the person who originated or gave existence to anything" and whose authorship determines responsibility for what was created.

Call to Action

God is the finisher of our faith. Trust the process and all that you have gone through, all you are going through and all that you must go through. Remember, there is a reason for everything. Every detail of our life is important for our story's outcome.

Though you cannot see it now, you will understand why you had to go through what you have gone through at the end of it all. Let God write your story of victory today; many lives are depending on it.

DAY 30 - LOOK! I'M GETTING WATER FROM A BROKEN WELL

Jeremiah 18:1-4 ESV

The word that came to Jeremiah from the Lord: "Arise, and go down to the potter's house, and there I will let you hear my words." So I went down to the potter's house, and there he was working at his wheel. And the vessel he was making of clay was spoiled in the potter's hand, and he reworked it into another vessel, as it seemed good to the potter to do.

I have come to realize that it is easy for us to tell people to trust in God. I often encourage people to trust in God, and when I tell them, I mean it, especially when they are going through a rough time. I encourage people because it comes naturally, and it is my gift. Encouraging people gives me joy and allows me to feel fulfilled as if I am walking in my purpose. When I can sit with someone or talk to them over the phone and minister to their spirit, it is refreshing. When I get calls or speak with persons when they need my help, sometimes I am going through a rough time myself. There are times I feel pressed out of measure, and I do not necessarily want to be on cheerful terms with God. However here comes the anointing and the Word, and there I am encouraging away as if nothing was wrong with me. As soon as I am through, I go right back to the state I was in because, at that moment, I was just a vessel that God wanted to use.

The benefit of helping others while you are struggling is rewarding because while you talk about God's goodness, it provides an avenue for your healing. While I'm helping others, I do get help, but there are times when I must go directly to God for myself. It gives me the joy to help others in whatever way possible because I know that,

He gives the desire, and He places the urge. The Holy Spirit does the prompting. Jesus is the one that saves; He is the one that keeps, He is the one that satisfies, and He is the one that provides. Some vessels that are broken can still be used depending on how they are broken. There are some vessels that, even though they are broken in some areas, they can still hold water or any other substance.

Some persons are broken but can still pray the fire of God down. Some persons are broken but can sing under the anointing and bless people's hearts. Some persons are broken, but they can preach the Word, and lives are changed. Some persons are broken, but they can still operate in the power of God's anointing. Your state of brokenness is not final; God will eventually gather your pieces and put you back together again. There are just some tasks that we have to do on behalf of God's kingdom that can only be done effectively in a state of brokenness. There are times we do things for the sake of Jesus Christ, but all the glory is not rightly attributed to Him at the end of the day. When you find yourself in a broken state, and the Lord uses you even in your current position, there will never be a place for you to glory in yourself when the task is achieved. All the praise will be given to God because for what you have just accomplished, it could not have been only you, but God was working in you and for this reason, He will rightfully get the glory He deserves. When turned into art, broken pottery can be some of the most beautiful things when it is put back together again. When we are broken, and God puts us back together again, we are more beautiful than we ever were, stronger, and more confident. Because we have been in a broken place, we understand what it feels like to fall apart, and because of this experience, we do our very best to avoid being broken to a certain degree again.

God requires brokenness, but the brokenness He needs is the one that will draw us nearer to Him voluntarily, willfully, and more open. He says,

*"A broken and a contrite heart he will not despise (Psalm 51:17 KJV). He healeth the broken in heart, and bindeth up their wounds **(Psalm 147:3 KJV)**.*

He is strong in your broken state, His grace is sufficient, and He will reach down to restore you. There is a place of brokenness that will drive us away from God, which is caused by being drawn away by our lusts and entice, walking outside of God's will for our lives. Self-inflicted brokenness will not help us, especially if it was not God's intention for us to have been broken in that season or time in our lives.

Brokenness does not last forever.

We all will experience different seasons in our lives where we will face all sorts of trials that life will throw at us. There are times that we will feel happy, sad, broken, whole, lost, discouraged, abandoned, loved, etc. However, the best part about this is that trouble only lasts for a while, but joy will come with the morning light.

Call to Action

Do not despise your seasons of brokenness; instead, embrace it because God can do more with you broken than when you are whole.

DAY 31 - WHO AM I REALLY?

Psalms 139:14 KJV

I will praise thee; for I am fearfully and wonderfully made: marvellous are thy works; and that my soul knoweth right well.

Sometimes we must face moments of doubt and uncertainty about who we are so that we can be truly vulnerable and open before God. What this vulnerability brings is the opportunity for God to,

> *"...grant you, according to the riches of his glory, to be strengthened with might by his Spirit in the inner man; That Christ may dwell in our hearts by faith; that we, being rooted and grounded in love, May be able to comprehend with all saints what is the breadth, and length, and depth, and height; And to know the love of Christ, which passeth knowledge, that we might be filled with all the fullness of God **(Ephesians 3:16-19 KJV).***

The moment we accept this truth, it will cancel all uncertainties about who we are in God. I must say that while in past years I would not have been able to talk with much confidence about myself, I now have realized, one that allows me to speak with much assurance and confidence that I truly love myself. Without any doubt, I can boldly declare that I belong to God. I would never use this medium as a means of self-glorification, but to give thanks to God for the work He has been doing in me and to encourage someone who may be in a similar position as I once was. I speak with much heart conviction that I love who I am and who God is molding me to be.

I do not need to feel intimidated by anyone anymore, nor do I need to compare myself with anyone. I am learning to embrace my flaws and weaknesses that make me who I am. I have lived a life of inferiority for so long that it took many rigorous processes to get me at this place of self-acceptance. God never gave up on me, even when I lived and breathed negativity about myself. I loathe who I was. I tried in so many ways to harm myself, but God would never allow it. He placed very genuine people in my life that would take the time every day to remind me of who I am. Somehow, they were able to see so many things in me that I never knew existed. Even though it took a while for me to accept what they often say, over time, as I read God's Word and communicated with Him through prayer, that is when something began to unfold in my heart, and I dare to say it was the truth of God grafted with His love.

I have no room in my life to glory in myself or whatever accomplishments I may have received. I consider myself blessed and favored by the Almighty God. There are many things I do not need to pray for that God provides. For example, I am not a hair-orientated person; whether long or short, I accept it - but God sees fit without me doing anything to my hair to cause it to grow. I am not hung up about having the perfect voice. I hardly consider myself a singer, but I see how God has blessed my voice to sing praises unto Him over the years. He provides clothing more than I need; He blesses me with a job that I did not apply or was qualified for; if I get sick, I don't even have to pay for my own doctor's visit. There are days when I get weak, and sometimes without praying, God would strengthen me. It demonstrates that God loves me, and I dare not doubt it again this day. There is a lot about my life that remains a mystery to me, and when I try to find out, I get knocked straight down on my knees in prayer, then at that moment, I'm reminded that whether I know it or not, God has a plan for me its end is purposeful and expectedly good.

My convictions about life are strong because my mode of operation is solely based on faith, living life knowing not where it will take me, waking up every day not knowing what it will bring but trusting God that through it all, He knows what He is doing. I am a Godchild! I am a daughter of the King, no doubt about that. I know for sure that a God with great taste fearfully and wonderfully made me. I appreciate my Maker, and I vow to serve Him until the end of my days, even into eternity always. I know many persons are in a place of doubt about who they are, and the plans God has in store for their life. Trust me when I say it's easy for us to speak like Gideon when God called him to deliver the children of Israel from the hands of the Midianites, Gideon said,

> *behold, my family is poor in Manasseh, and I am*
> *the least in my father's house* ***(Judges 6:15 KJV).***

In the sight of the Lord Gideon was a mighty man of valor (courage, bravery, boldness, fearless). Still, he was blinded by his insecurities, current state of life, and the family he was born into. He failed to see who he was in the sight of God. Many of us struggle with our self-image and people's perception of us, even our family's expectations to carry on the family name and legacy. I implore you to stop this instance! Examine your life; look in the mirror at the person looking back at you. Are you happy with your image? Are you walking in God's purpose for your life? Do you live with the truth of God's Word concerning you, that you are a mighty woman, man, boy, or girl of valor? People's perception of you is not important. What is essential is how God sees you and what His Word says concerning you.

*"Listen, O coastlands, to Me, And take heed, you peoples from afar! The LORD has called Me from the womb; From the matrix of My mother He has made mention of My name **(Isaiah 49:1 KJV).***

Call to Action

Each morning you go wake up look in the mirror and tell yourself;

- I am sufficient in God
- I am loved.
- I take comfort in belonging to God.
- My past does not define me
- I will not be ashamed

- God's mercy will not abandon me

- My heart is happy.

- I have found life in God

- God has great plans for me

- I am blessed

- I am strong and courageous.

- I will not give up.

DAY 32 - OH LORD! I HAVEN'T PRAYED IN A LONG TIME

1 Thessalonians 5:17 KJV

Pray without ceasing:

A life void of prayer is a life void of oxygen in which you will eventually die. An excerpt from an article posted https://www.unimedliving.com/living-medicine/medicine-and-living-medicine/the-importance-of-breathing.html states that;

"The human body can survive 3 weeks without food, 3 days without water, but only 3 minutes without air – unless you are one of those freaky free divers, which I'm assuming you are not. Without air, the brain starves of oxygen, normal bodily functions cease to exist, and essentially, we die. That makes breathing high on the priority list for human life. However, for most of us, we don't stress or worry about breathing, whether there will be enough air to breathe or even how we breathe, until we have a lung infection or an illness of the lungs, limiting or compromising our ability to breathe.

Prayer for a believer is like breathing. If we stop, it is inevitable that we die spiritually. For some of us, we do not worry about prayer or the importance of praying for our spiritual man's upkeep until we find ourselves in various kinds of helpless situations where we are unable to get out of by ourselves. That is the time when prayer becomes of vital necessity to us.

The absence of prayer is like a whirlwind. Can you imagine how catastrophic that would be? It uproots everything in its path and throws them out of place from their original position; the absence of prayer does precisely that in a believers' life. The absence of prayer means a lack of stability and the nonexistence of a secure foundation. We recount the illustration given in the Word of God about the foolish man who built his house upon the sand. The moral of which describes those who hear God's Word and do not take heed, and the wise man who built his house upon a rock representing those who hear God's Word and takes heed.thereof **(Matthew 7:24-27 KJV)**. A rock is a solid formation from the earth; it is very fixed and unmovable. Whenever foundations are being laid, the stone is a significant component and asset to its upbringing in any form of building infrastructure. The sand has no substance or solidity, so anything built or placed upon it can suffer the likely chance of being destroyed.

Jesus Christ is our immovable rock and our secure foundation. ***Isaiah 28:16*** states;

> *"Therefore thus says the Lord God, "Behold, I am laying in Zion a stone, a tested stone, A costly cornerstone for the foundation, firmly placed. He who believes in it will not be disturbed (KJV).*

Prayerlessness allows you to let down your guard. You become weak, fearful, vulnerable, and open to the enemy. Your mind is now left open and unguarded. Safe thoughts are now at risk of being attacked and replaced by negative thoughts. You find that the presence of God seems to bring liberty but a burden no longer because of the guilt that consumes you. As we have a right, coming to the throne no longer appears to be bold or easy for us, and this ought not to be so. The Word of God tells us in *Hebrews 4:16*

> *"Let us therefore come boldly unto the throne of grace, that we may obtain mercy, and find grace to help in time of need (KJV).*

When prayer ceases to become a committed lifestyle, your life becomes full of torment; your thoughts are provoked, sleep is gone away from you, and sin becomes almost easy to commit because of the unrest in your Spirit. When prayer does not guard the mind, it becomes an easy task for unfiltered thoughts to surface and take over your mind. The mind is a battlefield. It is with the mind that we serve God. In "*Romans 7:25* Paul said,

> *"I thank God through Jesus Christ our Lord. So then with the mind I myself serve the law of God; but with the flesh the law of sin (KJV).*

A prayerless life means that you are putting your spiritual life at great risk. What prayer does is that it forms barriers in our lives against the enemy.

Isaiah 59:19 tells us,

> *"So shall they fear the name of the LORD from the west, and his glory from the rising of the sun. When the enemy shall come in like a flood, the Spirit of the LORD shall lift up a standard against him (KJV).*

For the standard to be raised, we have to pray. When we fail to pray each day, we will begin to lose faith. Prayer contributes significantly to the strengthening of our faith. When we fail to pray as we are presented with situations or temptations daily, what we once believed as a fact about the ability of God's power, love, and grace to deliver us, suddenly becomes questioned, and the Apostle James warned us about being of two minds. ***James 1:8***

> *"A double minded man is unstable in all his ways (KJV).*

We must pray so that our faith can be strengthened. Each time we pray, and the Lord answers our prayers, it motivates us to pray more because we believe that once the Lord did it before, He can do it again, and this is faith in action the confidence we achieved through praying. Sometimes prayer can seem to be a hard thing to do, and that is because we lack the full understanding of how to pray. When we do not know how to pray, we ask God to teach us how to pray as the disciples did. There are times when you fall on your knees, or your face before God, overwhelmed by the pressure of the situation, and all you can do is groan. Did you know that is a form of prayer?

> *(Romans 8:26 "Likewise the Spirit also helpeth our infirmities: for we know not what we should pray for as we ought: but the Spirit itself maketh intercession for us with groanings which cannot be uttered (KJV).*

Therefore, we are not alone. We need to have the Holy Ghost; without the Holy Ghost, we will not have someone interceding on our behalf in the Spirit.

Jesus was and is our most remarkable example of a life lived in prayer. Prayer should not seem like a burden; that would tell us setting aside time to talk to our acclaimed lover would be a burden to you. Jesus never seemed to be burdened because He had to pray; instead, prayer was how He took care of the problems He had to face. Jesus prayed about everything. The bible might not have recorded every instance when He prayed. Still, we can be confident that He did live a life of prayer, taking a prayerful approach to every situation. Even throughout Jesus' suffering, one would think that He would not pray but to question His Father, complain, or take a sabbatical in prayer until the suffering was passed.

Nevertheless, He prayed even more through His suffering. We saw the intense moment with Jesus in Gethsemane. Even while He was on the cross, in the face of death, taking His last breath, He was still praying.

A prayerless life is a defeated life. Take it from me - I too used to live this kind of life.

Call to Action

Pray without ceasing. When you wake up, or before you go to bed, while walking, cooking, cleaning, washing. Pray while you are going through your midnight hour. Pray while you face pressuring circumstances, when you are on the mountain top or in the valley. Let prayer be the air that you breathe.

Proverb 24:16 NIV

For though the righteous fall seven times, they rise again, but the wicked stumble when calamity strikes.

It would be almost impossible for me to recount how many times I have failed throughout my life. My reaction towards failure was always negative. I never once tried to think positively about not accomplishing what I had set out to achieve; that was due to my ignorance of how important and necessary it is to fail. What! Did you say that failure is an essential component of life? Yes, you have read right. Sometimes we have to go through extensive failure before we can strike the mark of success. Constant failure, however, does not mean that you are a failure. You are considered a failure the moment you stop trying. Many of the world's most successful businesspersons had told their stories of how they had failed more times than they could admit before they were able to achieve success in their field of business. Many have conceived ideas that are multi-billion-dollar industries today.

According to https://invst.com/2016/08/24/15-celebrities-who-failed-to-succeed/ ***Thomas Edison.*** *One of the most important inventive minds of the 20th century was told by his teachers that he was "too stupid to learn anything." His teachers' predictions seemed to ring true, as Edison was fired from his first two jobs for not attaining a suitable level of productivity. Interestingly enough, being shunned from the working world was his ticket to success. Free from the handcuffs of societal standards, Edison's creative genius was* *unleashed: He went on to hold more than 1,000 patents and invented world changing devices including the phonograph, electrical light bulb – which he failed at developing nearly 2,000 times – and a movie camera.*

Colonel Sanders. *Before finding his seat on the throne as "The Colonel," Harland David Sanders was fired from dozens of jobs – both in and out of the food industry. His quest to deliver fried chicken goodness to the people of America took him across the country looking for someone to see his vision and sell his chicken. Finally, a business deal in Utah proved that his recipe truly was finger lickin' good, and thus Kentucky Fried Chicken was born. KFC is now one of the most popular food franchises in the world, and has over 18,000 locations.*

Failure is an inherent part of any journey to find success. Stopping at the first, tenth, twentieth, even fiftieth run-in with rejection or failure can mean you are selling yourself and your dreams short. When we talk about failure, we often think about something that we have set out to achieve but failed to accomplish. Nonetheless, I would like to provoke your thoughts about when we fail as Christians. There were many imperfect men and women in the bible who failed miserably but were used mightily by God.

> *To fail from time to time is only human, but to be a "failure" is when we are defeated by failure, refusing to rise and try again. Christians sometimes*

*believe they should be immune to failure by virtue
of their relationship with God, but the truth is that
God often allows us to fail for a variety of reasons.*

*Job 14:1 says, "Man born of woman is of few days
and full of trouble (KJV)."*

That doesn't say "unbelievers" or "the ungodly." It says man born of woman. What does that mean? Everyone. Life is full of trouble, even for those who belong to God through faith in Christ. We are to expect it. This means God does not promise life to be without problems, sorrow, and, yes, failure, just because we believe in Him.
<u>https://www.gotquestions.org/Bible-failure.html</u>

When we fail, we are reminded in the scriptures that God can keep us and, in the end, present us faultless.

*"Now unto him that is able to keep you from falling,
and to present you faultless before the presence of
his glory with exceeding joy,* **(Jude v24 KJV).**

When Jesus saved us, He knew that even after the work of salvation had begun in us, we would have moments of failure in our lives. Jesus knew that some of us would fall back into old habits that we have been delivered from, and some of us would have been ensnared into new habits that would form strongholds in our lives.

Yet, while we were reveling in sin, Christ died so that we would have the opportunity through Him to live freely without guilt and condemnation. What I am trying to bring across is that _we give up too quickly the moment we fail_. As Christians, we are the first to write ourselves off when we mess up or fail to meet a required mark, forgetting the kind of God that we serve. His stance on failure is different from our worldly view, and as such, He sees failure as an opportunity to show Himself strong and help us through our difficulties. Some of us perceive failure as the diagnosis of death because of this; many persons have left the church to this day because of something they did, and were unable to receive God's forgiveness.

They conclude that God does not love them anymore because they have failed; therefore, there is no use for them in His house. Too many times, I thought that about myself and was tempted to leave the church. On different occasions, I went to church upset with myself for failing God I could not truly give myself into worshipping Him because I told myself that God would never want a failure like me even to open my mouth to give Him praise. I thought to myself that He was even displeased with me being in His house. That however was far from the truth. Beloved, the truth is He was saddened that I felt that way and doubted His love for me even in my most horrific state. I think that Elijah could attest to how I felt because he, too, felt as if he had failed God.

Elijah had just had a "mountaintop experience" in defeating the prophets of Baal on Mt. Carmel. Fire had descended from heaven, the people of Israel acknowledged the Lord, and the false prophets

were all put to death. But that experience was followed by an episode of fear and failure in Elijah's life: the prophet was afraid and ran for his life from Queen Jezebel. The reason is made clear in 1 Kings 19:1–2: "Ahab told Jezebel all that Elijah had done, and how he had killed all the prophets with the sword.

Then Jezebel sent a messenger to Elijah, saying, 'So may the gods do to me and more also, if I do not make your life as the life of one of them by this time tomorrow.'" This death threat caused Elijah to flee a day's journey into the wilderness (1 Kings 19:4). At one point Elijah was so discouraged that he desired to die: "And he asked that he might die, saying, 'It is enough; now, O LORD, take away my life, for I am no better than my fathers'" (verse 4). In response, the Lord sent an angel to bring the prophet food and drink both before and after he slept. After the rest and nourishment, Elijah took a forty-day journey to Mount Horeb to meet with the Lord (1 Kings 19:6–8).

When I first read this passage, I could not understand why Elijah would feel the way he did. He just did this great work for the Lord. How could one little threat possibly dissuade him? What was astounding about all of this was God's response towards Elijah's actions. You see, God knows what we need in times of failure or when we mess up. Jesus knows how to get us back to the place where He is our hope and strength. Much like God's responsive attitude of love shown towards Elijah, so is His responsive love demonstrated towards us when we fall short.

Even though this is true, it does not stand in opposition to God's love for us. Scripture tells us;

We can learn from our failures. When we fail, we are constantly reminded of our imperfections. Some may view that as a bad thing, but we must always be in remembrance because then we will see how much we need God, His help, and His direction for our lives. The negative influence of failure produces discouragement for some, while for others, it produces hope. Each time we work towards achieving something and fail; this gives us a building block.

Each time you face rejection or disapproval, and you are told that you are not qualified enough, not intelligent, needy, or that you will never make it; your ideas or writing content will never cut it; those are building blocks of what is considered the start of your success. Use these cruel insults and setbacks as steppingstones and building blocks to construct a solid foundation on which you can stand. Build until you have reached your desired mark of success. All those who had gone before you were all rejected at some point, they all failed numerous times, but they used those experiences to build a better version of the ideas they originally had until they reached perfection.

We have not yet reached the place of perfection where we will be free from sinning or fighting the war raging inside us. Yes! We were saved and living with the hope and promise of a better life, eternal life, but until we leave this earth, we will have to fight, experience failure, rejection, sorrow, and a whole host of misfortunes until the Lord comes.

> *"Wherefore, take heart we are not fighting a losing battle, Seeing then that we have a great high priest, that is passed into the heavens, Jesus the Son of God, let us hold fast our profession. For we have not an high priest which cannot be touched with the feeling of our infirmities; but was in all points tempted like as we are, yet without sin. **(Hebrews 4:14-15 KJV).***

Call to Action

Each time you fail, lay that block down, learn from your mistakes, and take another step up from that place or despondency. Failure is not final. Failure is not the diagnosis of death.

DAY 34 – FACING REJECTION

1 Peter 2:4 NLT

You are coming to Christ, who is the living cornerstone of God's temple. He was rejected by people, but he was chosen by God for great honor.

Rejection can be as painful as the death of a close friend or a loved one. When someone is rejected, they are unwanted, not accepted, abandoned, castaway, or disapproved of. Everyone is susceptible and can become a victim of rejection. Someone at some point in time has rejected us all. We can experience rejection from our families, friends, relationships, in the workplace, at school, and in the church. Not everyone processes rejection the same way; but it can become a useful teacher to us all. Sometimes we have to face rejection more than once before we can finally realize that we can do better and we deserve better. Because of this truth, we can safely say that what we are reaching after or whom we are looking to can never compare to what is really in store for us. As it is written,

> *"Eye hath not seen, nor ear heard, neither have entered into the heart of man the things which God hath prepared for them that love Him." (1 Corinthians 2:9 KJV).*

It is amazing how little we settle for as children of God in our daily lives. We walk and live oblivious to our true worth and value as royal priesthoods, peculiar people, the praised of God's glory, joint heirs together with Christ, the redeemed, the salt, and the light in this broken world. Christians today are settling in abusive marriages and relationships that do not give praise to God, working in different jobs that belittle their standards, accepting things from persons to fulfill their needs in return for sexual favors. They are afraid of and do not want to face rejection. I remember all too well my moments of rejection from my family, friends, and relationships that I was engaged in.

I knew what it was like to settle as it was the life I lived for so long before God saved me. I suffered and was a victim of sexual abuse at the age of 12, which led to the loss of my virginity. After that and other events, I was unable to love myself, and from that time onwards, I lived a life of promiscuity. I was held against my will more times than I would like to admit, pressured into doing things I was not comfortable doing. I did all this out of fear and the thought that I was nothing good or of value. I tried committing suicide so many times; I was broken, felt unloved, and emotionally abandoned. All this took place while living in a family home, and they had no idea.

I wanted to feel loved and be loved, and I did not feel that way at my home. My mom was working hard to provide for us. My dad was always miserable and quarrelsome. My sisters and I would argue, so I did not feel like I truly belong. Low self-esteem and negative thoughts dominated my life, and my fear of rejection drove me to settle because I did not want to feel rejected again. Today I am a better person now than I used to be. How did that happen, you might ask? Simple, God saved me. I was introduced to someone who, like me, was rejected, but He overcame and paved the way for me to learn from past mistakes, forgive all who have wronged me and live a guilt free life through Him. Jesus is the perfect example for us to follow. His word has brought me sweet consolation and has changed my life for the better.

According to https://unlockingthebible.org/2016/03/dealing-with-rejection-through-the-gospel/

Jesus did experience rejection, quite a bit of it, actually. That's the beauty of the dual nature of our Savior. Being fully God, he chose to be brought low into the humanness of suffering. So every facet of Christ's life on earth was touched by rejection. Jesus faced rejection from family members. (John 7:5 KJV). Jesus faced rejection from his community. (Matthew 13:54-58 KJV) Jesus faced rejection from people who once claimed to love him. Christ, in his God-ness, predicted both Judas' betrayal and Peter's denial. He saw it coming. But his humanness still experienced the hurt. Jesus was "troubled in his spirit" as he foretold of Judas (John 13:21 KJV). Think about it.

He had just washed the guy's feet a few verses earlier, symbolizing the laying down of his very life for him. Peter, who professed his love and commitment to Jesus more ardently than any other, would reject even an association with him in a matter of hours. Sudden, total, heartbreaking rejection…yes, Jesus felt that. Jesus faced rejection from his Father. The night of his arrest, Jesus was "very sorrowful, even to death" (Matthew 26:38 KJV). He was in such anguish that he started to sweat blood (Luke 22:44 KJV). I think it was more than thoughts of the approaching physical pain that put Jesus in this state.

I think it was the knowledge that he would soon be separated from and abandoned by his Father. As he hung on the cross dying, Jesus cried out, "My God, my God, why have you forsaken me?" (Matthew 27:46 KJV). It's interesting that he didn't ask, "Why I am I in such pain?" or "Why do I have to endure this?" He asked, "Why have you forsaken me?" Sometimes, in our thoughts of Christ's death and what it did for us, we overlook what it did to him. His Father, with whom he was in a constant communion of love from before time began, was suddenly forced to withdraw that love and turn his back because of our sin that covered Jesus as he died. Do you think Jesus had ever

The healing that comes from knowing that our Savior stood in a place of rejection that we who are saved would never have to suffer that dreadful feeling again is remarkable and life changing. We no longer have to settle for less. We do not have to process rejection as the end of all things good. When others reject us, Jesus reminds us in ***John 15:18-19***

> *"If the world hates you, ye know that it hated me before it hated you. If ye were of the world, the world would love his own: but because ye are not of the world, but I have chosen you out of the world, therefore the world hateth you (KJV).*

Call to Action

Do not write off being rejected as something terrible. God has more extraordinary things in store for you. If you face opposition or rejection in any way, it is God's way of pointing you to better opportunities

DAY 35 - HOW DO I RESPOND IN SEASONS OF DARKNESS?

1 Peter 2:9 KJV

But ye are a chosen generation, a royal priesthood, an holy nation, a peculiar people; that ye should shew forth the praises of him who hath called you out of darkness into his marvellous light:

I have found myself saying this "I don't want to be a false representative of Christ on this earth." As Christians, our actions can be misleading at times, and we must never forget that we are continually being watched. Jesus says;

we are the light of the world, a city that is set on a
hill that cannot be hidden (Matthew 5:14 KJV).

Light illuminates, and because this is a dark world, those who live in darkness will easily identify us. Our actions and our speech should never betray us or cause anyone to think twice about us or whom we represent. There will be times when we are tested. Sometimes, we will be required to face seasons of darkness to know whether we reflect the true light. Situations will present themselves to misguide us in this life. For that reason, we want always to be sure that as ambassadors, we represent the truth of Christ written in His Word and that our light in this world will influence, bring hope and draw men unto our Lord and Savior Jesus Christ.

After Jesus was baptized in the river Jordan by John the Baptist, the bible said in *St. Matthew 3:16*

"And Jesus, when he was baptized, went up
straightway out of the water: and, lo, the heavens
were opened unto him, and he saw the Spirit of God

descending like a dove, and lighting upon him (KJV):

The spirit of God immediately led Jesus into what I refer to as a season of darkness to be tempted by the devil. During this time, Jesus fasted for 40 days and night. According to ***Matthew 4:1-11***

"Then was Jesus led up of the Spirit into the wilderness to be tempted of the devil. And when he had fasted forty days and forty nights, he was afterward an hungred. And when the tempter came to him, he said, If thou be the Son of God, command that these stones be made bread. But he answered and said, It is written, Man shall not live by bread alone, but by every word that proceedeth out of the mouth of God. Then the devil taketh him up into the holy city, and setteth him on a pinnacle of the temple, And saith unto him, If thou be the Son of God, cast thyself down: for it is written, He shall give his angels charge concerning thee: and in their hands they shall bear thee up, lest at any time thou dash thy foot against a stone.

Jesus said unto him, It is written again, Thou shalt not tempt the Lord thy God. Again, the devil taketh him up into an exceeding high mountain, and sheweth him all the kingdoms of the world, and the

Satan is revealed in ***Revelation 12:10 (KJV)*** as the accuser of the brethren. An accuser is a person who says that another person has done something wrong; especially that he or she has committed a crime. To accuse is also to charge with a fault or offense. An accuser is always looking for someone to blame, which is exactly what Satan was trying to do with Jesus. This season of darkness that Jesus was experiencing caused Him to feel weak, vulnerable, hungry, and, might I say, tired. Being in this state is the perfect place that the devil would love to have us, a place where our defense is weak and susceptible to his destructive elements.

However, while Jesus was in such an open position, His response to the devil's temptation was based solely on God's Word. Jesus could have easily given up in such a dark season of His life. Just after been saved, He could have walked away, but He held out to the end, and the key take away from Jesus' entire season of darkness is this *"Man shall not live by bread alone, but by every word that proceedeth from the mouth of God."* There was no room for Satan to accuse Jesus of being a false representation of light.

Satan could not say that Jesus' actions were misleading because Jesus gave him no reason to be able to accuse Him. Can this be said of us when we are experiencing our seasons of darkness? After many failed attempts to sway Jesus, Satan left, having been defeated, and straightway angels came and ministered unto Jesus. The result of overcoming His season of darkness rewarded Him with much power, strength, and glory in that the prophecy spoken afore time was fulfilled which says,

> *"The land of Zebulon, and the land of Nephthalim, by the way of the sea, beyond Jordan, Galilee of the Gentiles; The people which sat in darkness saw great light; and to them which sat in the region and shadow of death light is sprung up. (Matthew 4:15-16 KJV).*

I reiterate what I said earlier in the opening passage that light illuminates, and because this is a dark world, those who live in darkness will readily identify us. I have had days when I am pressed out of measure, and to be honest, I tend to get angry and frustrated easily. Sometimes, when people would try to reach out to me, I would snap at them or find myself arguing over simple things, cursing with such passionate rage. We all have our weaknesses, and well, anger is one of mine. The devil knows this because I am tested in this area quite often. Sometimes I am victorious, and sometimes I am not. My siblings would say, *"Nuh you say you a Christian and a cuss so!"* Friends, I feel so bad afterward to have lost my cool like that in front of my unsaved siblings, and having them say that to me was heartbreaking, worse if in my head I was reciting scripture pertaining to the situation and not exercising it at the same time. Have you ever had that experience?

You are in a particular situation, you are being tempted, and the scripture is reverberating in your mind what you should do, and then you end up failing. Well, I have been there. It is often said that many persons will not take up a physical copy of the bible to read. We are the bibles that they are reading, watching to see if we are truly living what we are preaching, especially to them.

Call to Action

Be encouraged by the scriptures that tell us how we ought to conduct ourselves as ambassadors, children of the Most High God.

- *Walk in the wisdom of God as you live before the unbelievers and make it your duty to make him known. Let every word you speak be drenched with grace and tempered with truth and clarity. For then you will be prepared to give a respectful answer to anyone who asks about your faith. (Colossians 4:5-6 TPT)*

- *"Live such good lives among the pagans that, though they accuse you of doing wrong, they may see your good deeds and glorify God on the day he visits us."* **1 Peter 2:12 NIV**

- *And don't be intimidated by those who are older than you; simply be the example they need to see by being faithful and true in all that you do. Speak the truth and live a life of purity and authentic love as you remain strong in your faith.* **(1 Timothy 4:12 TPT)**

DAY 36 - MY SOON TO BE EX – DEPRESSION

I find myself frequently depressed - perhaps more so than any other person here. And I find no better cure for that depression than to trust in the Lord with all my heart, and seek to realize afresh the power of the peace-speaking blood of Jesus, and His infinite love in dying upon the cross to put away all my transgressions. - Charles Spurgeon

I am a fan of the Prince of Preachers - Charles H. Spurgeon. His sermons are so intoxicating, and his style of writing is simply outstanding. I am enthralled each time I listen to or read anything that he writes. However, even though he was such an anointed and gifted preacher, the great Spurgeon battled with depression throughout his life.

Spurgeon's battle with depression started when he was 24 years old. It was 1858, and Charles Spurgeon later recalled, "My spirits were sunken so low that I could weep by the hour like a child,

In reference to the Preacher Charles H. Spurgeon, though he is deceased, I admire his work, passion, and zeal for the Lord. Knowing that he battled with such a soul sickening disease as depression throughout his life and ministry made me think. For as far as I can recall from a child until this day, I have been battling depression. I suffered to the point of being sick physically, emotionally, sexually, mentally, and spiritually. There are days I would wake up sad, happy, crying, suicidal, weak, just a mixture of different feelings. If I pondered on my life for too long, I would get depressed, more so if I saw others thriving and I am going through a period of distress. There are days when I allow my insecurities to lead me astray, my fears to tell me what I can or cannot do, my shortcomings to stop me from moving forward, and my weaknesses to dictate my strengths. There are also days when I allow myself to sin presumptuously, my selfish will to get in God's way, low self-esteem to steer my confidence, and my anxieties to lead me in making impulsive decisions. I certainly never had it easy, and from time to time, thoughts swam in my mind about how I would survive. There are days when my doubts would cloud my judgments, my negative thoughts would steal joy from my life, and my shame in asking for help would make me full of pride. I have had times when my failures would dictate my outcome, and I would allow comparison to get the better of me. I would let my feelings generate a false sense of reality. I would allow my past to define me, people's perceptions of me to doubt the truth about who I was, and my relationships to get to a place of insanity. I would allow other people's success to make me feel less important to society and my flaws to paint a false hope that this is who I'll always be. All this was adding more weight to the depression I was already sunken in. When I was battling with depression, there are days when I would try to fight it but end up losing all energy and willpower, so I just lay down and accept defeat.

Like Spurgeon, who fought his depression with faith, I started to take baby steps towards wholeness over time. I love God, and that goes without question. You see, even though I struggled, I knew that it would have never been for long. I am finally getting freedom from these strongholds. I am daily revived by the uncompromising, unfathomable, genuine, forgiving, unconditional, everlasting LOVE of God. He knew that I would have been laden with all of these struggles even after He saved me.

Christ proved God's passionate love for me by dying in my place while I was still lost and ungodly! **Romans 5:8 (TPT).**

All this that Jesus did propelled Him to love me more, and He went a little further to say that nothing can separate me from His love.

"So now I live with the confidence that there is nothing in the universe with the power to separate us from God's love. I'm convinced that his love will triumph over death, life's troubles, fallen angels, or dark rulers in the heavens. There is nothing in our present or future circumstances that can weaken his love. There is no power above us or beneath us—no power that could ever be found in the universe that can distance us from God's passionate love, which is lavished upon us through our Lord Jesus, the Anointed One! **Romans 8:38-39 TPT**

You may be a victim of depression. I still get depressed from time to time, but I have found the answer. Like Spurgeon, I put my faith in the one true and living God. He knows what you are experiencing. He did it for others and is doing it for me. Therefore, He can do the same for you NOW! I believe God is bigger than all things. I believe He has given us all things pertaining to life and godliness. While we wait on Him to fulfill His promises concerning our lives, let us rejoice in Him who is faithful, the God who is our bedrock and our salvation. The God of all comfort, wonders, and Praise, He who reigns in the hearts of all men, Christ our redeemer, Christ our Lord and King. Let us crown Him with honor, glory, and Power. Let our hearts be humble before Him, and let our praises ring out, songs of victory and Hallelujah's praise blessed be His name. He reigns forever and ever more. He has purchased our pardon; now we are free. Praise God we are free. We must walk in Power and confidence. Because of the knowledge of our Lord and Savior Jesus Christ, WE KNOW WHO WE ARE.

He loves us, yes, He does, and those whom He loves He chastened. May our humbled hearts rejoice in Him, and our souls find rest in Him. We can face each day because He lives. What have we to render for all His benefits? Nothing but our lives a living sacrifice, our only worthy offering. We have nothing to fear because we are found in Him. He is the greater power that lives in us, the dynamic force that changes us, the armor that clothes us, our daily bread, our bread of life, and manna, which feeds us. Like the woman at the well, we will never thirst again. He is our fountain of living water. His wisdom satisfies us, His mighty hand guides us, and we lack nothing in Him, for we are filled with the abundance of His abiding love.

He lays us in green pastures. Our life is ordained, blessed, and prosperous. His Word is a lamp unto our feet and a light unto our path. Our life is in His hands, our future, our purpose, and our goals. Who we should become our desires, destiny – it is all in Him. His mercy is everlasting. His Grace covers us, His love constrains us, and His compassion enfolds us. What a God! Miraculous is He. I am so glad that Jesus loves you and He loves me. I'm so happy He cares, I'm so glad He sacrificed His life for us, we wouldn't have done what He did, felt what He felt, or suffered for the sins of humanity, but faithful is He who has called us and even so to the utmost Jesus saves. We are anointed, appointed, approved, and commissioned for this time. Let us not be ashamed of the gospel that has wrought our salvation, the gospel of Jesus Christ, it is the power of God unto salvation to them that believe.

Call to Action

Are you in an agonizing relationship with depression? Friend! You owe that bastard nothing! God has given you the gift of freedom; you are free from guilt and condemnation. The joy of the Lord is your strength. PUT AN END TO THAT TOXIC RELATIONSHIP NOW!

DAY 37 – BUILDING A RELATIONSHIP WITH GOD

1 John 4:10 NLT

This is real love—not that we loved God, but that he loved us and sent his Son as a sacrifice to take away our sins.

Building a genuine and intimate relationship with God is of utmost importance in this season of my life, and I will tell you why I refer to this present time and not since the time I became a born-again believer. My views on relationships were always based on my childhood experiences, and if you know my childhood story, you will see that they were not all very good experiences. I lacked the love I believe I was supposed to receive from my family. Well, not from my mom; I was always by her side. I love her very much, and I know she loves me too, but she was still busy, always working to provide for us, so there left little to no room for her to spend the time with me as she wanted to. Working and making ends meet was her way of saying, I love you every day, along with providing the necessities of life. In earlier times, I mentioned being sexually abused, which drove me into great distress. I lost my identity from a very early age, and my life was dominated by fear, low self-esteem, depression, and hatred for myself.

All the relationships I entered from that time on shattered whatever dignity I had left in me. My understanding of what relationship meant was me giving myself and proving myself to gain the love I lacked from my home and friends. I thought that if I did not do something for someone or have sex with a guy if he asked, then they wouldn't love me, and why should they? I mean, look at me! So repulsive and stupid, how could anyone ever love me? Those were the thoughts I lived with every day. Throughout high school up until the day I left, my life was a whirlwind of emptiness. I was in a relationship for three and a half years, and I had other guys talking to me on the side. I gave all of me while working at the same time to prove myself to earn their love, and to this date, I doubt if I have ever received what I pointlessly worked for. After I broke up with my ex-boyfriend of 3 1/2 years, I told myself I never wanted to be in a relationship again.

Now that you understand where my mind was regarding relationships let us fast forward to an entirely new time when I became a born-again believer. I heard so many things about God, the most famous line *"Jesus loves you."* "God sent His only son to die for your sins, no matter what you have done, who you are, or where you come from, you're accepted by God, He loves you very much, and He is inviting you into a relationship with Him." Hold up! A relationship? "Yeah, right". That was my reaction in my mind. Does God know who I am? How could God ever love someone like me, let alone even want to be in a relationship with me? It was hard for me to accept that Jesus loves me without having an ulterior motive. As the time progressed and I began to learn more about God and His love for me, I did well sometimes in accepting that okay; maybe God does love me. But! Yes, there's a but. There were days when my past came back to me and took over my mind, bringing its memories, railing accusations, guilt, and shouts of condemnation. I cried to the Lord to help me. Sometimes there was no response from Him. There I was in the dark, calling for God, and He was nowhere to be found.

Then you hear teachings that God will never leave you or forsake you, He is a present help in the times of trouble, that we should call on Him and cast all our cares on Him for He cares for us. Subsequently I question, how can God love me and He is not even helping me or answering me when I call to Him? Building a relationship with God was hard for me. Each time I did something wrong, it took me a long time to go to Him and ask for His forgiveness, although He invites us to

"come boldly unto the throne of grace, that we may obtain mercy, and find grace to help in time of need. ***Hebrews 4:16 KJV.***

I could not bring myself to believe that

"If we confess our sins, he is faithful and just to forgive us our sins, and to cleanse us from all unrighteousness. ***1 John 1:9 KJV.***

It was an overwhelming and hard truth to swallow. Therefore, each time I sinned or messed up one way or another, I did to myself what you called penance. Penance is the punishment inflicted on oneself as an outward expression of repentance for wrongdoing.

I would often inflict myself with pain because I thought for me to be forgiven and for God to still love me, I had to do something to prove my sorrow for what I had done. Each time I ended up coming short, I thought that God was displeased with me, and every time I did something right, I thought He would be pleased with me. It continued for a few years. I lived a lie concerning my relationship with God. Yes! He used me, I ministered into people's lives, I prayed some through to the Holy Ghost, I witnessed to persons, and they were saved. I was active in my assembly doing everything, but I had a legalistic relationship with God. I prayed and fasted all the time. I enjoy God's Word. I value it, yet even though convicted, I could not accept or understand this kind of love that God wants to give to me. A type of love that wants nothing from you in return, a love that will never abuse you, hurt you or cause you to live in fear, be jealous or for you ever to doubt or question the genuineness of its loyalty and faithfulness. A love that even if you blatantly walk away or turn your back to peruse your pleasures, it will chase after you, never letting you go or perish in danger. A kind of love that

> *"If I go up to heaven, you're there! If I go down to the realm of the dead, you're there too! If I fly with wings into the shining dawn, you're there! If I fly into the radiant sunset, you're there waiting!* **Psalms 139:8-9 TPT.**

Such love, such wondrous love that God should love a sinner such as I, how wonderful is love like this. Do you see why I had a hard time believing? My mind was saturated with the thoughts that I'm a nobody, and for the rest of my life, I will have to prove myself to people and give my body to men for me to be loved. The 14th day of March 2021 will mark six years since I accepted Jesus Christ as my Lord and Savior, and I spent many of those years living a legalistic lifestyle while having a shallow understanding of God's Grace. While some saw the coronavirus pandemic as the worst thing that has ever happened, it was the greatest, most vulnerable, eye-opening moment of my life. Throughout the entire pandemic, I was in a very dark place. The darkness was so thick I could feel every inch of it all around me, but it never consumed me. What? So how could that be something good? My dear readers, that season was God's way of preparing me.

"Yea though I was walked through the valley of the shadows of death, I feared no evil because God was with me. His rod and his staff they comforted to me. (Psalm 23:4 KJV).

As the year ended and gave birth to a new calendar year, I emerged from the darkness of 2020 and rose with the light and glory of a new season and a new beginning. It took me almost six years of being saved to breaking free from the lies of legalism, such as when people attempt to secure righteousness in God's sight, they do so by their good works. I also believe that you can earn or merit God's approval by performing the law's requirements, that my good works and obedience to God affect my salvation, and that I should focus on God's laws more than my relationship with God. In addition, I should keep external laws without a truly submitted heart and that legalism adds human rules to divine laws and treats them as divine. My breakthrough came from personally seeking God after becoming tired of inflicting myself with pain as punishment for my sins, trying to prove myself to God, working and beating myself against the wind. I didn't want to acknowledge it at first that I was a legalist, even after I heard so many preaching about this kind of mindset and lifestyle and having identified with everything that confirmed I was indeed living such a life.

Nevertheless, I learned this one thing throughout my life; there is strength in confession, restoration in repentance, and power in commitment to God. The moment I finally accepted that I was living a lie, I immediately went to God. Like David, I sought the Lord, and he heard me. One night I had a divine encounter with the Lord, and there He revealed to me how He felt about me. After such a wonderful experience, man, I felt as though I was walking in mid-air.

My confidence and faith meter skyrocketed. No one could tell me otherwise about God's love for me. Starting this year, it is the first in a long time that I can genuinely pursue my loving heavenly Father without the pestering distractions of my childhood and past. I find God so intriguing now; He is so sweet, oh my God. The closer I get, the more I lose the desire for the things I once thought I needed to be happy in this life. The things I once held as high priority have now become of little to no importance to me because I DESIRE HIM, I DESIRE JESUS CHRIST AND ALL OF HIM. I found all I need in him. Every void is filled, nothing missing; nothing lacking I found all I need in Jesus. Do not get me wrong, I have certainly not arrived, but I INTENTIONALLY take a step towards getting to know Him more through prayer and His Word each day when I wake up.

- I am encouraged by David's intense pursuit of God.

"O God of my life, I'm lovesick for you in this weary wilderness. I thirst with the deepest longings to love you more, with cravings in my heart that can't be described. Such yearning grips my soul for you, my God! I'm energized every time I enter your heavenly sanctuary to seek more of your power and drink in more of your glory. For your tender mercies mean more to me than life itself. How I love and praise you, God! Daily I will worship you passionately and with all my heart. My arms will wave to you like banners of praise. I overflow with praise when I come before you, for the anointing of your presence satisfies me like nothing else. You are such a rich banquet of pleasure to my soul. I lie awake each night thinking of you and reflecting on

198

how you help me like a father. I sing through the night under your splendor-shadow, offering up to you my songs of delight and joy! With passion I pursue and cling to you. Because I feel your grip on my life, I keep my soul close to your heart. Those who plot to destroy me shall descend into the darkness of hell. They will be consumed by their own evil and become nothing more than dust under our feet. These liars will be silenced forever! But with the anointing of a king I will dance and rejoice along with all his lovers who trust in him. **Psalms 63:1-11 TPT.**

- I am motivated by Paul's desire to want to know Jesus.

"But what things were gain to me, those I counted loss for Christ. Yea doubtless, and I count all things but loss for the excellency of the knowledge of Christ Jesus my Lord: for whom I have suffered the loss of all things, and do count them but dung, that I may win Christ, And be found in him, not having mine own righteousness, which is of the law, but that which is through the faith of Christ, the righteousness which is of God by faith: That I may know him, and the power of his resurrection, and the fellowship of his sufferings, being made

*conformable unto his death; **Philippians 3:7-10 KJV.***

God wants us to have a personal understanding of who He is. He wants us to seek Him so that we can come to the knowledge of the truth for ourselves. Having a personal relationship with God is to be known by God. Seek God for yourself. Let not man teach you about God. Let God teach you about Himself.

*"But the anointing which ye have received of him abideth in you, and ye need not that any man teach you: but as the same anointing teacheth you of all things, and is truth, and is no lie, and even as it hath taught you, ye shall abide in him.**1 John 2:27 KJV.***

I want to share a part of what the spirit of the Lord told me when He revealed His love for me.

- "Not every man can handle the intricacies of my ways, before the foundation of this world I have handpicked you before you were even formed in your mother's womb."
- "My yoke is easy, my burden is light, and I can assure you that I the Lord in me you shall find delight."
- "As you have read in the gospels, so shall be these last and closing days."
- "I have set you on the pathway to heaven, go, and sin not in thy ways."

- "As you travel along the path, though narrow it can be, flee from the devil, resist all things from him, and shun all his evil deeds."

- When you come to a place that you will be greatly tempted, call upon the Lord so that you will not do the things that could be prevented."

- "Remember you are not perfect so you will do things that are wrong, and when you do, I will not be mad but rather make you strong."

- "I am your daddy, and my love for you comes in all manner of ways."

- "If you are sad, I will be your smile on all your raining days."

- "If you are weak, I will bear you up in my arms; if you are cold and afraid, I will keep you safe from harm."

- "When the enemy comes to destroy you, I will stand in your place. I will shield you and protect you and forgive you of all your disgrace."

- "When the world thinks that you are mad for loving me, do not pay them any mind; only continue to love me until the end of time."

- "To them, they have no time to believe in the things that are unseen, but those things that can be plastered and put-upon big screens."

- "When your head swings low, I will cushion it into place. When you need a bedtime story, I will tell you of the heavenly race." "It was told to comfort you and remind you of the place you will go, only if you trust in me, follow me and leave this world below."

- "I cannot stop myself from loving you even if I try. I died for your sins, and I am glad my Father sent me to pay the price."

- "Encourage your friends on earth to put their trust in me; I don't just want to love you but to be involved with all who wants to be involved with me."

Call to Action

In your quiet time, take a few moments to answer these questions. Who is God to me? Do I desire Jesus?

DAY 38 - PURPOSE IS ON YOUR LIFE

Jeremiah 1:5 NLT

"I knew you before I formed you in your mother's womb. Before you were born I set you apart and appointed you as my prophet to the nations."

Everyone always told me that God has a plan for my life and that what I am going through is to fulfill God's purpose. Purpose! What purpose? All I know is that God has it out for me. There is no way this could be a part of God's plan for my life; this is meant to destroy me. This was always my response whenever I thought about my life, where I am, and the circumstances I faced each day. Let me give you a brief overview. Shortly after I left high school in 2014, my mom got a stroke that badly affected her. We took her to Kingston to be treated. I was encouraged by one of my sisters to apply for college. I took her advice because I did not think my mom was going to be this way forever. I applied to the Excelsior Community College and did my interview. I was accepted and was scheduled to start in September. In August, we returned to Montego Bay. I immediately began to prepare for school in the next couple of weeks. Bear in mind that I was not yet saved at that time. As the days drew closer for me to leave for school in Kingston, my mom was sitting on the veranda one evening. I took one look at her, and then it hit me!

I could not leave her in her state, so I called the school explained my situation, and asked for a deferral. That day my journey began. It would be almost impossible for me to write and explain all that I went through caring for my mom. Because I was not saved in the initial stage, I was always angry, bitter, and full of malice towards my situation, family, friends, life, and myself. I did not know anything about God or Him having a plan; I just looked at it as life choosing to be unfair to me and allowing everyone else to live their best lives. I was depressed often. I cried myself to sleep night after night, then wake up the next day in despair, wishing to die. My mom's illness grew worse. Every day something new developed. One day I grew so tired of my life that I decided I would end my life. Before that, a friend I met who was a teacher at my alma mater invited me to an Apostolic Church. I told him I would attend church with him, of course, I did not go. Immediately after, I soon forgot all about it. It was around the time I was on my way to commit suicide when I remember the invitation to the church out of the blues.

At that point, something changed within me, and I decided I was going to go to the Church that following Sunday. On the 22nd of February 2015, I walked into the King's Chapel United Pentecostal Church like a real evil badass rebel and left that day graciously filled with the Gift of the Holy Ghost. I was then baptized in Jesus' Name on the 15th day of March of the same year. My siblings and I grew up in a Baptist Church, so I did not have one ounce of clue or understanding about this Apostolic Faith. Please pay close attention because the things I'm about to say will be vital for you to understand my point at the end of this writing. The first day I visited the Church, I did not know where to go, so I just went to the first Sunday school class I saw, and that was the young adult's Sunday school. I was 17 years old at the time, and I should have been in the intermediate Sunday school class. However, nobody could have guessed I was 17 because I did not look my age. I looked very old and mature *(in sin)*, that is. After receiving the infilling of the Holy Ghost and being baptized, it is customary that all new converts be placed in the new convert's class. That is for persons who are newly saved where they feed you the milky aspect of the Word of God.

The new convert's class was for babies; there, we learned to crawl before we walked. However, when it came time to place me in the class, they placed me in the Senior high Sunday school class, I spent two years, and it wasn't easy. Remember, I was just saved. I didn't know anything about the apostolic faith, so I should have been where babies should be, and that's the new converts class but, God had a different plan, and I can say this now because back then, I honestly didn't understand. My whole process of growing up spiritually was complicated and backward. I ended up walking before I crawled. All my behaviors were learned, how I prayed, how I operated, everything. It was stressful because I messed up a lot, fornicated often, and drowned ever so often in my low self-esteem, and now, looking back, I can see where this contributed to me living a legalistic lifestyle.

In Senior High Sunday School, it was for young persons in their 20s. I was only 17 at the time. From an early point of being saved, I was involved in the church doing so many things, including taking part in different ministries. There was no space or time to breathe; I was just consumed with doing. That is why I lived a lie concerning my understanding and in my relationship with God. Now that you understand let us get back to where we left off. When I just got saved, I use to fast and pray every day. Prayer was like breathing to me, and fasting became a ritual over a time where I go without eating food. However, I can tell you I spent a lot of time in the Word. I have had experiences and encounters where God talked to me, showed me things, put me in a deep trance and minister to me, among other things. One of the things I sought God for was the situation with my mother. That day I locked myself away and began to pray. Not long into praying, the Lord showed me a vision. The Lord showed me a tree bent over in the vision as if it would almost break in two. Then He showed me a strong piece of wood shaped like the letter 'Y' that was placed by the tree to support it from breaking, and the Lord said to me in the vision I am that support for my family that is on the verge of breaking. I was still young in the faith, and for me, that was a big responsibility. How could God possibly think I could manage such a task when I can't even take care of myself? It was an uphill task, and I messed up so many times than I could count. I got into many arguments with my siblings and father. I could not see how God wanted me to take on such a responsibility.

Nevertheless, what I have come to learn is that if the Lord has called us to do something, He has already made the provisions necessary for us to accomplish such a task.

Take Joseph for example, this is a summarized version of (Genesis 37-50). Joseph's father made a coat of many colors for coat for him. This stirred up jealousy among his brothers. When Joseph was sent to a distant pasture one day to look after his brothers, they seize him, tore off his coat; throw him into a dry well. His brothers later sold him to the Ishmaelites as a slave and they carried him into Egypt. Joseph started to serve in the house of Potiphar. While serving under Potiphar, Potiphar's wife tries to seduce Joseph to sleep with him but Joseph refuses to dishonor his master, so the woman spreads a report that he tried to rape her and Joseph is placed in prison for something he did not do. In prison, Joseph is assigned to attend to the prisoners among who were two high court officials who were suspected of wrongdoing.

The two high court officials were tormented by dreams, the men ask Joseph for help. Joseph tells the cupbearer that he will be reinstated and the chief-baker that he will be hanged. Two years later, the cupbearer remembers Joseph when Pharaoh is unable to obtain from his priests a rational interpretation of two anguishing dreams. Joseph is summoned and predicts that after seven years of plentiful harvest, Egypt will suffer seven years of famine. Convinced, Joseph eventually gains the favour of the pharaoh of Egypt by his interpretation of the dream and obtains a high place in the pharaoh's kingdom. Joseph immediately began to put aside a fifth of the country's harvest. After seven years a murderous famine strikes, driving people from nations near and far to come to Egypt to buy grain. Among the famished, Joseph recognizes his brothers. Testing them to see if they have changed, Joseph is satisfied and reveals his identity. Finally reunited with his beloved brother Benjamin and his father Jacob, Joseph reconciles with his family, and Pharaoh invites them to settle in Egypt as overseers of his livestock.

Joseph suffered tirelessly from the hands of his brethren and the hands of those with whom he was sold. Anyone who does not understand how God works would say that He is a cruel God for allowing this to happen to such a young boy at age 17. He experienced unfairness, cruelty, betrayal, abandonment, suffering, all because the Lord gave him a dream, and he was zealous to share it with his brethren. They envied him for the plans God had for his life. They never encouraged him, neither did his father, so his brethren plotted against him to kill him, but instead, after the plea of one of his brothers, they sold him into slavery. *(Genesis 37:18-36 KJV)* if you read the entire account of Joseph's story, he trusted in God, through such difficult times in his life, he remained faithful to God through testing and trials. He had many opportunities to turn his back on God and to give up believing the dreams God had shown him.

He had the perfect opportunity to have slept with a woman. However, he held on to his integrity and his devotion to God. Through his hardships, his gifts were cultivated, he could interpret dreams, and he had a leadership spirit. His brothers intended to kill him, but after Joseph reconciled with them, he said, "***But as for you, ye thought evil against me; but God meant it unto good, to bring to pass, as it is this day, to save much people alive. (Genesis50:20 KJV).*** You might be wondering how all of this relates to me? Since taking care of my mom, I tried two more times to go to college, and it just did not work out. I started but could never finish because the responsibilities were hard to handle along with school demands. I have suffered a nervous breakdown twice, lack of sleep, poor health problems, working on and off, balancing responsibilities while trying to carry on with my personal life, and many other things. Of course, I thought that this was to kill me.

How could God put me through this? I thought that my life was a complete mess because I didn't get to go to college, everyone seems to be living their best lives, I couldn't go out as I would want to, how could this have possibly been God's will for my life? That is what I use to say back then because I did not understand, but now its all clear to me, and like Joseph, I had to experience all those hurt, pain and suffering to fulfill God's plan. Today my mother is baptized in Jesus Name and is yet to receive the Holy Ghost. My sister and niece are baptized and filled. I am working on the rest of my family. I am in a job that I am not qualified for, and I am at peace taking care of my mom as opposed to when I started. There were many things in my life and my family that was wrong. Many things that would have caused it to break but God, through His infinite wisdom and sincere love, saw it and saved me for such a time as this. I am still taking care of my mom. It gets a bit challenging from time to time, but God has equipped me with all that is necessary to endure, and if He is doing it for me, He can do it for you.

Call to Action

We are not to regard suffering as a strange occurrence but rather as a sign of God's work in our lives. You must patiently wait with joyful expectation for the manifestation of God's full and divine plan for your life. Are you wondering or in doubt, whether or not God has a purpose for your life? Whether your present suffering is for a reason? Yes! Yes! And Yes! He is currently at work on your behalf right now. God is preparing you. Now, it will not be joyous,

> *"But He knows the way that I take [and He pays attention to it]. When He has tried me, I will come forth as [refined] gold [pure and luminous]. (Job 23:10 AMP)*

DAY 39 - A SUSTAINER IN YOUR SEASONS OF NOTHINGNESS

Isaiah 43:2 NLT

"When you go through deep waters, I will be with you. When you go through rivers of difficulty, you will not drown. When you walk through the fire of oppression, you will not be burned up; the flames will not consume you

These times are nothing but trying times. You are hard-pressed to the fullest of your human extent, and it would almost feel like life itself in a moment may come to an end. I do not know about you, but my days of living on reserve have been long gone. What I have come to realize is that we must care for ourselves holistically. No one will do it for us, so we must take ourselves up in hand. There is never a day, whether good or bad, that we should exclude God from the regime of our daily lives. We are not perfect, and sometimes God's involvement to the extent we would allow should be more. Yes, you've rightly read there are days that we are the ones who would tell God how to operate and the extent to which He should work in our lives, but friends, God does not work like that of this, I am sure.

I cannot imagine life without God. Well, I can, but even in my most imaginative state, I still would not be able to comprehend the magnitude of loss and emptiness, purposelessness, and inadequacies that I would feel. I have seen how dull life can become. A few months ago (in 2020, to be exact), I thought I was at a good place in my relationship with God, only to find myself in a place of dryness like a desolate land dried and cracked. The Corona virus pandemic has shown up my flaws. I was sure about the flaws I knew about that those might have been my only major imperfections. But low and behold, the skeleton had finally popped out of my forced closed closet. Now the truth has been revealed. It can no longer be concealed.

Going to church was a cover for the things I seldom wanted to face, the issues I had to deal with, and the strong effect of my selfish disgrace. Old habits resurfaced, old desires awaken, now I am suddenly surrounded with old baggage and new ones asking to get in on a piece of the action. Bible left untouched, prayer closet filled with cobwebs and dust, the altar where my reasonable sacrifices were offered now started to rust. Frustration set in, stressed, depressed no wonder my life had been such an awful mess. Everything about my walk with God that could have been shaken was left aloof; misery set in and left me wondering just what to do.

I did not even bother to consider where God would be at that time because I knew that even in my many failed pre-planned attempts to reach Him, He was standing right there waiting for me to acknowledge that I was empty and that I need Him. There have been times where I sat down and presumptuously sinned even when my conscience was eating me alive. I did this because I was looking for an escape from my cycled life. I know it was wrong, but I could not bring myself to stop, and I may be a monster to say this, but through it all, I never doubted God's love for me at all. I was sitting and waiting, hoping and praying that God would help me because I could not help myself. Of a truth, all I could do was look to the hills from whence cometh my help

"I cried unto the Lord with my voice, and he heard me out of his holy hill. I lay me down, and I slept, I awake for the Lord sustained me. I declare that thou oh Lord are a shield for me, my glory, and the lifter up of my head **(Psalm 3:3-5 KJV).**

Even though life is hard, trust me, I am a fighter I will not quit. The difference is that I have God as my guide. I am His child and just like that! Jesus covers me under the multitude of His wings. I am loved and accepted because I alone cannot bring myself to win. I have fought the fight, and the victory I have won by whatever means I have overcome is by Jesus Christ and His shed blood. I am not afraid anymore; I do not need to be because I know that He watches me even in my state of nothingness. I am grafted in His hands; His eyes continuously behold me. God has not forgotten me. He knows my name, my desires at present may have subsided, but they can rise again. Rekindle again little fire burning in my heart; pour the anointing oil continuously to give me that fresh start. I know that I will make an impact, and the world will see my glorious mark. I live to reflect the life of Christ; I am an ambassador, branded for the cause that men will come to know the one who hung on a tree who died for our forgiveness and to set us free.

You might have been in that same position I once was, but God can keep you through whatever season you may be facing in your life. Everything about my life is a miracle and testament to the glorious power of God. That is why I can write about the goodness of God. He has not allowed the unfair but necessary circumstances of life to overwhelm me to the point of insanity or death. Instead, He kept me, and He can keep you.

"When you go through deep waters, I will be with you. When you go through rivers of difficulty, you will not drown. When you walk through the fire of oppression, you will not be burned up; the flames will not consume you (Isaiah 43:2 NLT).

You are never too far for His hand to reach you.

"Surely the arm of the LORD is not too short to save, nor his ear too dull to hear (Isaiah 59:1 NIV).

You have the strength through God to rise from any situation. Just reach out to God.

Call to Action

Perhaps at the moment, you are feeling low in your spirit. You may feel down and feel like God has somehow forgotten about you, but I can tell you that He is present in your midst. Stretch your hands by faith and reach out to God in prayer. You are not beyond the hand of God! You are not beyond His reach. His hands stretch far; it reaches long and wide enough to encompass you and save you.

DAY 40 - CHOOSE FAITH IN SPITE OF YOUR SUFFERING

1 John 5:4 KJV

For whatsoever is born of God overcometh the world: and this is the victory that overcometh the world, even our faith.

The bible stated that Job was a perfect and upright man who feared God and turned away from evil. He was blessed with wealth greater than anyone who lived in the land of Uz. He served God daily and consistently, offering up sacrifices each day, even for his family, praying, and worshiping God. Until one day, the bible declares,

"that there was a day when the sons of God came to present themselves before the Lord, and Satan came also among them. And the Lord said unto Satan, Whence comest thou? Then Satan answered the Lord, and said, From going to and fro in the earth, and from walking up and down in it. And the Lord said unto Satan, Hast thou considered my servant Job, that there is none like him in the earth, a perfect and an upright man, one that feareth God, and escheweth evil? Then Satan answered the Lord, and said, Doth Job fear God for nought? Hast not thou made an hedge about him, and about his house, and about all that he hath on every side? thou hast blessed the work of his hands, and his substance is increased in the land. But put forth thine hand now, and touch all that he hath, and he will curse thee to thy face. And the Lord said unto

Satan, Behold, all that he hath is in thy power; only upon himself put not forth thine hand. So Satan went forth from the presence of the Lord. (Job 1:6-12 KJV).

The long and short of it is that Satan wasted everything that Job had: his animals, his children, his home, his properties, even his health. Now one would ask, how can God be so cruel to allow this to happen to someone who daily worships Him, who does his best always to put Him first and glorify Him? Nevertheless, what he was currently facing sparked a response of faith and gratitude that caused him to say,

"Naked came I out of my mother's womb, and naked shall I return thither: the Lord gave, and the Lord hath taken away; blessed be the name of the Lord" **(Job 1:21 KJV).**

In any trial that we face, we don't "Just" get up with an automated faith response. It is not all the time that we will regard our situations with faith being our first reply. Job chose to trust God. He decided to look beyond all that has just happened. He chose not to be sided with his wife after she told him to curse God and die. Honestly, anyone in his position would be tempted to turn their backs on God and curse him. Nevertheless, he chose to ignore his wife, and he decided to respond to his situation by faith.

His response was much like Jesus when He was on the cross. Instead of focusing on is the current situation, the bible says that,

*"who for the joy that was set before him endured the cross, despising the shame, and is set down at the right hand of the throne of God" **(Hebrews 12:2 KJV).***

Jesus saw His victory over the cross by placing faith in the father long before it ever happened, so this blessed faith gave Him the assurance and strength needed to endure the cross and despise the shame at that moment. Whatever and wherever we find ourselves in life, no matter what or where it may be, remember that as humans, one of our tendencies is that we are not going to answer or solve our problems firstly by choosing faith automatically. We tend to get worried or react with non-faith responses first. Nevertheless, in any given situation, you must choose faith. Believe that things will work out in your favor. Choose to look ahead of your current situation and believe that it will get better. Choose to believe that God is able.

At the end of all the hurt, pain, misery, depression, persecution, resentment, hate, brokenness, hopelessness, and emptiness, choose to believe that it will get better. There will be glory after this. There will be victory after this. God will turn it around. He will bring you out. God will move in your situation. He will heal you when the doctors give up on you. He provides during a recession. Have faith in Him. He will come through. God specializes in impossible things. He loves to move when all hope is lost so that He can show Himself strong on your behalf. Do not give up. He will come through for you.

Can I tell you about four men who were on the verge of dying? Some would even say that they were already dead men walking. However, these men made a decision of faith that brought to pass a prophecy the Lord gave unto to the prophet Elisha. 2 Kings 7 speaks about four leprous men who sat at Samaria's gate. There was a famine in the city of Samaria. Because of their condition, they were considered outcasts, so one of them said to another,

> *"Why sit we here until we die? If we say, We will enter into the city, then the famine is in the city, and we shall die there: and if we sit still here, we die also. Now therefore come, and let us fall unto the host of the Syrians: if they save us alive, we shall live; and if they kill us, we shall but die.*

> *2 Kings 7:4 KJV And they rose up in the twilight, to go unto the camp of the Syrians: and when they were come to the uttermost part of the camp of Syria, behold, there was no man there.*

> *For the Lord had made the host of the Syrians to hear a noise of chariots, and a noise of horses, even the noise of a great host: and they said one to*

Therefore, they told the porter of the city, who then informed the King. The king sent his men to find out if what these leprous men said was true and so came to pass the prophecy concerning the famine and the provision of food for Samaria. The incredible thing about this was that these men were in a dreaded condition, my God! They were next to death, but the faith-based decision they made, the walk of faith they took, made the camp of Samaria's enemy to hear a mighty army. I want us to know that our decision of faith is vital for us to overcome the world: ***and this is the victory that overcometh the world, even our faith (1 John 5:4 KJV.***

Call to Action

Can you believe what the Lord will cause your enemy to hear if you decide to take a walk of faith despite your present circumstances right now? I want you to stand up on your feet and take a walk by faith today. You know what you are experiencing at home, you know what you are facing on the job, you are stuck in a low place, your bills are due, you lost your job during the pandemic, and all hell has broken loose in your life. Declare in the atmosphere today that it is well. Believe God by faith today regarding your mountain.

ABOUT THE AUTHOR

 Daniela Aaliyah Blake the last of eight siblings was born and raised in the beautiful city of Montego Bay, Jamaica. She is an ardent Christian who lives by the principles of God's Word. She considers herself to be much like the biblical character – David – as they both share similar callings: Godly-purpose, love of God's precepts, interests, struggles, family situations, faith, and beliefs in God. Much like David was a man after God's own heart, so too is Daniela, a woman after God's own heart. Even as David was an articulate writer and enjoyed expressing himself to God through carefully, well thought out words, Daniela is the same.

Daniela's zealousness about anything she does is seen in her ambition and drive, her excellent communication skills, as well as her creativity and passion. The one thing therefore, that outweighs all these attributes that she possesses is her unfeigned love for the Lord. As Paul rightly puts it in *1 Corinthians 15:10* *"But by the grace of God I am what I am: and his grace which was bestowed upon me was not in vain;"*

She is an active member and Vice President for the Youth Department at the King's Chapel United Pentecostal Church. She spends her time helping and encouraging others and works well with young people. She is eager to share her passion and love for God with the whole world, and to be an inspiration to everyone that she comes into contact with.

For speaking engagements and/or book signing:

Email: daniellablake845@gmail.com
Instagram: *dan.i_royal*
Facebook: **Daniella Blake**